GLOBALISATION ·

A Calculus of Inequality

Perspectives from the South

Edited by

DENIS BENN

and

KENNETH HALL

Ian Randle Publishers

Kingston

First published in Jamaica 2000 by
Ian Randle Publishers
206 Old Hope Road, Box 686
Kingston 6

ISBN 976-637-019-2 paper

A catalogue record of this book is available from the
National Library of Jamaica

Cover and book design by Robert Harris
Set in Orchid 9.5/14 x 27
Printed and bound in the United States

Contents

Foreword

I am extremely pleased to introduce this volume on globalisation, given the importance of the phenomenon in shaping contemporary international economic relations.

During the past decade, no country has been able to escape the influence of this phenomenon which has had a particularly profound impact on the developing countries, including the small island developing states of the Caribbean served by the University of the West Indies.

The developing countries are all too conscious of the significance of globalisation in shaping the lives and destiny of their people as traditional preferential arrangements, previously accorded to them in recognition of the disadvantages deriving from the undeveloped and undifferentiated nature of their economies, are being dismantled and replaced by the principle of reciprocity in the context of an increasingly liberalised and competitive global economy. Indeed, these principles are being systematically codified in various international economic and trade agreements being put in place, most notably, those embodied in the Uruguay Round agreements and others being negotiated within the framework of the World Trade Organisation (WTO).

At the same time, the process of globalisation has conferred immense power on the transnational corporations, located mainly in the developed world, but with increasingly global reach, and has also strengthened the power and influence of the IMF, the World Bank and the WTO as a triad of forces shaping the principles which govern the global economy. This development has been accompanied by a conscious policy on the part of the developed countries to reduce the role of the United Nations which has traditionally served as an important instrument in support of the development efforts of the developing countries.

Needless to say, while globalisation has provided opportunities for increased trade and investment, mainly for those countries with a developed productive capacity, it has led to the emergence of significant power asymmetries and economic inequalities between the countries of the North and those of the South, and has, in effect, reinforced the historically determined inequalities which have traditionally governed the relations between the two groups of countries. Indeed, large parts of the developing world are threatened with marginalisation as a result of the impact of the forces which currently influence the operation of the global economy.

Despite its negative consequences for the majority of the developing countries, the process of globalisation has been accompanied by a growing literature in the North espousing the virtues of globalisation and the related concept of economic liberalisation which has served as its legitimising philosophy. This has resulted in the imposition of an intellectual hegemony by the North in terms of the propagation of ideas which influence current approaches to both domestic and international economic policy.

In contrast, there has been a dearth of literature from the South challenging the assumptions of globalisation and economic liberalisation, despite the significant impact of the phenomena on the economic fortunes of the developing countries.

Yet, disaffection for globalisation has grown and is spreading. The Asian crisis had demonstrated serious structural weakness in the global economy deriving from volatile capital markets - leading to calls from several quarters for a 'new financial architecture'. As the century ended, Seattle dramatically highlighted both the dangers of rampant liberalisation and the refusal of the world's majorities to be press-ganged into it. In short, while powerful ideological forces still preach liberalisation and globalisation as economic gospel, people on many fronts in all countries are unconvinced and unconverted – and some are in rebellion.

It is now clear that future international economic negotiations will still take place in the context of globalisation, but the way ahead in those negotiations will be more open to intellectual questioning of the premises that have driven them in recent times. At the South Summit in Havana recently, the leaders of the South demonstrated their capacity, and readiness, to challenge the prevailing orthodoxy and reiterated their determination to influence the outcome of the negotiations on global economic issues.

This volume is very timely in that it offers perspectives from the South on globalisation and economic liberalisation, highlighting the particular consequences of these phenomena for the developing countries. As such, it will make an important contribution to the global debate on the merits and demerits of these processes which are destined to influence the future of humankind in a manner that few previous developments of this nature have succeeded in doing.

I hope that the book will not only inform developing countries about the impact of globalisation on their economic fortunes and therefore inspire suitable policy responses on their part but also enlighten the North about the consequences of current approaches to globalisation. In doing so, it could also serve as a catalyst for reorienting international economic policy with a view to obviating the adverse economic impact of such policies on the developing countries and lay the foundation for the creation of a more equitable and enlightened international economic system in the service of humanity.

Sir Shridath Ramphal
Chancellor
University of the West Indies

Preface

Globalisation has, in a sense, become the dominant theme of our age, with significant implications for the development prospects of the developing countries. As such, the developing countries face the urgent task of formulating suitable strategic responses to the challenges posed by globalisation.

It was for this reason that the University of the West Indies organised, in February 1999, an international symposium on 'Globalisation – A Strategic Response from the South' in order to discuss the central issues posed by globalisation and to identify possible responses that could be adopted by the developing countries. The symposium brought together academics, policy makers from regional organisations and participants from international organisations. I would like to express our appreciation for the financial assistance provided by UNDP in support of the symposium.

This volume contains papers which were either presented at the symposium or prepared specifically for the occasion. Taken together, they provide important insights into the phenomenon of globalisation and therefore make an important contribution, from the perspective of the developing countries, to the ongoing debate on the subject.

I therefore commend the volume to policy-makers and academics as well as members of the general public, given the profound impact of globalisation on all aspects of contemporary society.

Professor Kenneth O. Hall
Pro Vice Chancellor and Principal, Mona campus
University of the West Indies
May 1, 2000

Acronyms and Abbreviations

ACP	Africa, Caribbean and Pacific
ACS	Association of Caribbean States
APEC	Association for Pacific Economic Co-operation
CACM	Central American Common Market
CARICOM	Caribbean Community
CARIFORUM	Caribbean Forum
CBI	Caribbean Basin Initiative
CEMAC	Economic and Customs Union of Central Africa
CLAA	Caribbean Latin American Action
CMEA	Council for Mutual Economic Co-operation
CU	Customs Union
DAC	Development Assistance Committee
DR	Dominican Republic
EAC	East African Economic Community
ECCB	Eastern Caribbean Central Bank
ECDC	Economic Co-operation among Developing Countries
ECLAC	Economic Commission for Latin America and the Caribbean
EEC	European Economic Community
EU	European Union
FDI	Foreign Direct Investment
FTAA	Free Trade Area of the Americas
G7	Group of 7
G15	Group of 15
G 24	Group of 24
G77	Group of 77
GATS	General Agreement on Trade in Services
GATT	General Agreement on Tariffs and Trade
GDP	Gross Domestic Product
GEF	Global Environment Facility
GNP	Gross National Product
ICAO	International Civil Aviation Organisation
ILO	International Labour Organisation

IMF	International Monetary Fund
IPR	Intellectual Property Rights
LAC	Latin America and the Caribbean
LDC	Least Developed Countries
MERCOSUR	Mercado Común del Sur (Southern Cone Common Market)
MFI	Multilateral Financial Institutions
MFN	Most Favoured Nation
MAI	Multilateral Agreement on Investment
MNC	Multinational Corporations
NAFTA	North American Free Trade Area
NAM	Non-Aligned Movement
NGO	Non Governmental Organisation
NIEO	New International Economic Order
NTM	Non Tariff Measures
OAS	Organisation of American States
ODA	Official Development Assistance
OECD	Organisation for Economic Co-operation and Development
OECS	Organisation of Eastern Caribbean States
OPEC	Organisation of Petroleum Exporting Countries
PAHO	Pan American Health Organisation
PSOJ	Private Sector Organisation of Jamaica
REPA	Regional Economic Partnership Arrangements
RNM	Regional Negotiating Machinery
SADC	Southern African Development Community
SAP	Structural Adjustment Programme
SELA	Latin American Economic System
SICA	Sistema de la Integración Centro Americano (Central American Integration System)
SIDS	Small Island Developing States
TCDC	Technical Co-operation among Developing Countries
TNC	Transnational Corporation
TRIMS	Trade Related Investment Measures
TRIPS	Trade Related Intellectual Property Rights
TWN	Third World Network
UN	United Nations
UNCDP	United Nations Committee for Development Planning
UNCTAD	United Nations Conference on Trade and Development
UNDP	United Nations Development Programme
UNIDO	United Nations Industrial Development Organisation
USSR	Union of Soviet Socialist Republics
UWI	University of the West Indies
WHO	World Health Organisation
WTO	World Trade Organisation

Introduction

During the past decade or more, the phenomenon of globalisation has exercised a profound influence on the structure of international economic relations. At the same time, the concept has generated considerable debate and controversy between those who proclaim its merits and those who point to its negative consequences for the economies of the developing countries.

Although the terms are conceptually distinct, globalisation has become inextricably linked to economic liberalisation in the context of the recent evolution of the global economy. The latter concept, which is underpinned by neo-classical economic principles and which emphasises increased private sector development, the primacy of market forces and unfettered trade liberalisation, provides the theoretical rationale for the creation of an increasingly integrated and interdependent global economy. It therefore serves as the legitimising ideology of globalisation.

Viewed in this context, globalisation may be seen as a natural outgrowth of the economic policies applied under IMF/World Bank sponsored economic stabilisation and structural adjustment programmes implemented during the 1980s which reoriented the economies of the developing countries towards increased integration into the global economy. The programmes were premised on an explicit abandonment of the traditional approach to economic policy based on the notion of a developmental state orchestrating widespread interventions in the economy. Instead, they asserted the primacy of market forces and an increased role for the private sector in the economic sphere as the basis for ensuring an optimal allocation of resources, with a corresponding retrenchment of the functions of the state, based on a minimalist conception of government.

The proponents of globalisation which, as stated earlier, is founded on the philosophical bedrock of neo-liberalism, have argued that the removal of trade barriers and the creation of a liberalised global trading regime will produce substantial benefits through a significant increase in global trade, variously estimated at US$250 to US$500 billion a year, although some critics of globalisation have argued that the actual benefits from trade expansion under a liberalised regime are likely to be much more modest, perhaps ranging from US$150 to US$250 billion a year. More importantly, however, they have pointed to the fact that, even assuming a significant expansion of global trade, the benefits of such an expansion are likely to be unequally distributed, with the bulk of the benefits accruing to the developed countries which have a sufficiently developed productive capacity to compete effectively in the global economy. On the other hand, the developing countries, particularly the least developed countries in Africa, given the undifferentiated nature of their economic structure and their relatively underdeveloped productive capacity, are likely to suffer significant economic marginalisation as a result of globalisation. In fact, it has been estimated that the majority of the countries in Africa, mainly the least developed countries, are unlikely to benefit significantly from the Uruguay Round agreements in view of the low level of manufacturing in the overall composition of output in their economies.

Notwithstanding the reservations expressed by its critics, the process of globalisation has continued apace and has in fact become formalised in the series of agreements concluded during the Uruguay Round of multilateral trade negotiations, most notably the Trade Related Investment Measures (TRIMS), the Trade Related Intellectual Property Rights (TRIPS) and the General Agreement on Tariffs in Services (GATS). What, in effect, these agreements have done is to 'multilateralise' a number of principles espoused mainly by the developed countries and imposed upon the developing countries. This is best illustrated by the TRIPS agreement which is based largely on a restrictive US national standard that is much more favourable to the owners rather than the users of technology. This is not surprising, given the fact that the negotiating brief of the United States on the subject was heavily influenced by corporate lobbies, in particular the major transnational pharmaceutical corporations, which pushed for the adoption of the measures to prevent the unauthorised use of their patents. While, therefore, the principles embodied in the Uruguay Round agreements have been projected as 'neutral' and 'universal' in content, they essentially reflect the interests of the developed countries, with modest concessions to the developing countries.

What is also significant is the fact that the new international 'rules of the game', which have been incorporated in the various multilateral trade agreements concluded during the Uruguay Round, are enforceable by the World Trade Organisation (WTO), which was established in 1995 at the end of the Uruguay Round to serve as a forum for ongoing trade negotiations and as an instrument to monitor compliance with the agreements concluded under the Uruguay Round. This latter function has major implications, since countries are subject to sanctions for failure to conform to the provisions of the various agreements which, in many cases, impose a number of onerous responsibilities which many developing countries are not capable of fulfilling without significant external assistance.

Notwithstanding the negative impact of a number of the provisions contained in the Uruguay Round agreements on the majority of the developing countries, the developed countries, in keeping with the logic of neo-liberalism, continue to press for a new round of trade liberalisation in areas such as competition policy, procurement, labour and environmental standards on the ground that further liberalisation in these areas will bring additional benefits to all countries. Needless to say, the developing countries have been sceptical about the advantages to be derived from a new round of trade negotiations, and therefore a majority of these countries are opposed to the new round on the terms proposed by the developed countries, before undertaking a thorough review of the impact of the agreements previously concluded during the Uruguay Round.

In addition, the developing countries have been concerned about the undemocratic nature of the negotiating process adopted within the WTO, whereby, under the so-called 'green room' process, only a small number of countries are invited to participate in the negotiations on particular issues, to the exclusion of the majority of member countries of the organisation – particularly the developing countries. This approach is therefore perceived by the developing countries as lacking in transparency and therefore of questionable legitimacy. This consideration was a major factor in the rejection of the efforts of the developed countries, during the WTO ministerial meeting in Seattle in December 1999, to push through an agreement on a new round of trade negotiations; although a number of other elements were involved in the so-called 'debacle in Seattle', some of which, such as the US labour movement and environmentally–oriented Non Governmental Organisations (NGOs), embraced different, and sometimes conflicting, agendas, despite being united in opposition to the WTO.

The experience of the East Asian crisis, together with the 'Seattle debacle', has prompted increased questioning of the validity of the assumptions which underpin current approaches to globalisation and economic liberalisation. As a result, a number of critics of globalisation have called for the 'strategic' integration of the developing countries into the global economy. In this approach, integration into the global economy would occur on a selective and phased basis in terms of the liberalisation of those sectors which are capable of competing in the global economy. Strategic integration is also premised on the development of a suitable institutional capacity to manage the process of liberalisation, particularly in respect to short-term capital flows, which have a considerable potential to generate financial instability.

It is also argued that, given the underdeveloped nature of their economies, developing countries would need to defend the principle of special and differential treatment and other suitable economic arrangements in order to ensure their viability in a rapidly globalising world.

More generally, based on the East Asian experience and its adverse economic impact on the developing countries, there is a general tendency in some quarters, including mainstream academic circles in the developed countries, to revisit the assumptions of globalisation and economic liberalisation and to argue in favour of a more interventionist approach to economic management in order to ensure international economic stability and the equitable distribution of the benefits of the process of globalisation. In a sense, the opposition is not so much against globalisation *per se* but against the current *approach* to globalisation, which is seen to be inimical to the interests of developing countries.

Indeed, in this context, the assumptions of a resurgent neo-classical economic orthodoxy which underpin globalisation and economic liberalisation, tend to be seen as above challenge. However, viewed in terms of the evolution of economic theory, neo-liberalism gained a similar ascendancy during the late nineteenth and early twentieth century, only to be discredited following the 1929 stock market collapse in the US, which was seen as a conspicuous example of market failure and which therefore gave rise to the interventionist approach embodied in Keynesianism.

Moreover, many of the developed countries which currently espouse a policy of economic liberalisation have historically pursued highly protectionist policies at an earlier stage of their development in an effort to stimulate the growth of their productive capacity. Particularly noteworthy is the example of the United Kingdom which pursued for centuries a policy of mercantilism, as illustrated by the adoption of the famous Navigation Acts of the seventeenth century, to consolidate its control over the colonies in an imperial division of labour between the metropole and the colonies which was clearly biased in favour of the former. It was only after it had undergone an industrial revolution in the nineteenth century, which was funded in part from the profits derived from centuries of mercantilism, that the United Kingdom became a major advocate of free trade during the second half of the nineteenth century, as was evidenced by the activities of Richard Cobden and John Bright, the leaders of the Anti-Corn Law League who, in proclaiming the merits of free trade, essentially reflected the interests of the rising industrial classes in Britain. A similar pattern of economic development was evident in the United States which, in the early years of the Republic, and indeed for most of its history, subscribed to pro-protectionist Hamiltonian economic principles, notwithstanding the triumph of a Jeffersonian conception of governance.

It should also be noted that the Smoot-Hawley Trade Act, adopted in the US in 1930, is generally regarded as one of the most restrictive trade measures ever imposed by a country. In other words, the enthusiasm for free trade in both countries was inspired largely by the development of a productive capacity capable of competing in the global arena and, more importantly, a perception of the national advantages to be gained from the pursuit of such a policy.

Given its extensive ramifications, it is clear that globalisation will continue to provoke debate on its merits and demerits. The papers presented in this volume deal with various aspects of the phenomenon, ranging from an examination of its philosophical foundations to more practical concerns, such as the formulation of counter strategies as well as with specific issues which have arisen in the context of the negotiations taking place in the WTO.

Against this background, Branislav Gosovic, in his article entitled 'Intellectual Hegemony in the Context of Globalisation', points to the fact that during the past decade the developed countries have succeeded in imposing an intellectual hegemony based on the assertion of a neo-liberal ideology which reflects their geo-political and economic interests. This in turn, he argues, has led to the virtual intellectual disarmament of the developing countries, thus preventing them from effectively advancing an alternative development philosophy capable of countering the assumptions of neoliberalism. In Gosovic's view, the paradigm imposed by the North has tended to downplay the relevance of concepts such as development, equity, self-reliance and exploitation and has also sought to sideline the United Nations (UN) organisations and agencies, particularly UNCTAD which has historically played an important role in articulating the development needs of the developing countries. Moreover, the intellectual dominance of the North has strengthened the role of the international financial institutions (and, more recently, the WTO), which have imposed a number of restrictive multilateral norms and conditionalities on the developing countries. He therefore argues that the developing countries have an important responsibility to challenge the intellectual hegemony of the North by positing an alternative vision of development. He believes that, in order to do so successfully, the South would also need to seek to restore the primacy of the UN in the economic sphere and also to establish an alliance with academics and other groups in the North which are sympathetic to the position of the South, as prerequisites for the creation of a truly democratic international community.

Clive Thomas, in his article entitled 'Globalisation as Paradigm Shift: Response from the South', takes the position that although some commentators have argued that globalisation is not really new, he believes that the world is experiencing an unprecedented transformation and therefore the current expansion of globalisation represents a genuine paradigm shift. In this context, he points to 'the dynamic interconnectedness of contemporary global society' which he sees as far more intense than it has ever been. As he puts it, 'more than in any previous era, human endeavours are conceived, designed and implemented as global projects'. Thomas feels, however, that the emphasis on unrestricted market-led development, which is explicit in the neo-classical theoretical underpinnings of globalisation, can be destabilising and contradictory and can also lead to polarisation and conflict. He therefore asserts the need for the political and social determination of global markets as a necessary condition for pursuing a successful programme of globalisation. In terms of practical strategies, he feels that the South would need to advance constructive options from which programmatic formulations on the way forward might be forged. More specifically, he advocates a three-pronged strategy based on support for the UN, and in particular the extension of its influence over global social and economic affairs; the promotion of South-South co-operation; and the strengthening of regional and sub-regional co-operation, and even bilateral relations, between the countries of the South. Thomas believes that there is danger that under current approaches to globalisation the market will be seen as an end in itself. He also feels that there is a need to maximise the benefits from the operation of the Transnational Corporations (TNCs), which have become dominant actors in the global arena, with a corresponding emphasis on efforts to minimise the social costs of their operation. To do so, it will be necessary to ensure that they operate within a political and social framework not of their own making but of citizens and their preferred political institutions. Thomas believes that if this were to be done, globalisation would be made to serve the needs of all humanity, rather than humanity serving the interests of the few.

In the paper entitled 'Globalisation and the North-South Divide: Power Asymmetries in Contemporary International Economic Relations', Denis

Benn argues that, although globalisation is facilitated by technological change, it is essentially a product of conscious economic policy on the part of the developed countries in support of their economic interests, based on the creation of expanded opportunities for trade and investment on a global scale. He also argues that the current approach to globalisation, which is reflected in the principles embodied in the multilateral trade agreements concluded during the Uruguay Round, most notably the TRIMS, TRIPS and GATS agreements, together with the operation of the WTO itself, has led to significant power asymmetries between North and South and also growing income disparities between the two groups of countries. He points out that the process of globalisation has been accompanied by an increasing shift in physical production to the developing countries by transnational corporations from the North, in an effort to maximise the returns on capital through the exploitation of cheap labour and in the reaping of increased value to the North derived from the sale of the products produced by such labour at considerably increased prices. This trend is also likely to reinforce, in the long run, the existing economic disadvantages faced by the developing countries in terms of the operation of the global economy. However, Benn notes that the East Asian crisis and the negative impact of globalisation on some developing countries have raised serious questions about the validity of the assumptions regarding the efficacy of unfettered market liberalisation which underline globalisation. Moreover, he argues that the market cannot by itself guarantee economic stability and social equity, therefore some form of multilateral intervention by governments is necessary to ensure economic rationality in the operation of the international economic system. He feels that the developing countries should seek to systematically deconstruct the neo-classical economic theory underlying the current approach to globalisation with a view to formulating an alternative development paradigm aimed at ensuring a more rational ordering of the international economic system.

In dealing with the topic, 'The South in the Era of Globalisation', John Ohiorhenuan identifies the impact of globalisation in respect to trade, finance, and investment with special reference to the expansion of the role of the TNCs in the process. According to Ohiorhenuan, the growth of globalisation has led the developed countries to challenge the relevance of the traditional North-South divide, which they see as a legacy of the Cold War, and to argue instead that international relations should be based on the concept of a partnership between North and South. He also points to the declining role of the state in the new dispensation. Ohiorhenuan believes, nevertheless, that an intensified programme of South-South co-operation could form the basis of a strategy to ensure the effective integration of the developing countries in the global economy.

In focusing on 'The Recent Systemic Crisis and the Management of the International Financial System', Manuela Tortora argues that the economic vulnerability of Latin American countries cannot be treated as a purely regional problem, since the phenomenon of globalisation has had a major economic impact on the region. She also emphasises the 'systemic' nature of the East Asian crisis, in terms of its impact on international capital markets, trade flows, and recession, and also its implications for the stability of the international financial system. Tortora therefore calls for an integrated approach to international financial management and emphasises the need to give priority attention to the establishment of an early warning system and the provision of an adequate level of development financing. She also emphasises the need to put in place an effective system of international financial governance, although she considers that such an endeavour would encounter a number of obstacles and, therefore, the redesign of the current international financial architecture will not be easy, given the various interests involved and the need to secure widespread political consensus on the subject.

In his paper on 'Globalisation and Counter Globalisation; The Caribbean in the Context of the South', Norman Girvan distinguishes between globalisation as an ideological term and globalisation as a substantive process. In his view, the former implies the organisation of the world according to the principles of neo-liberal economics and in accordance with a presumed inevitability of the process leading towards the formation of a single world economy, society and culture driven by technology and the transnationalisation of investment and finance capital. For Girvan, globalisation is based on a coherent political, institutional, theoretical and ideological order and embodies a set of prescribed practices and a convenient and easily recognised label. In contrast to these assumptions, Girvan posits the notion of counter-globalisation, which implies a critique of the market-oriented, corporate-led globalisation process and which advocates alternative ways of managing national and international exchange. Counter-globalisation therefore challenges the neo-liberal assumption that markets are 'free and fair' and that they lead to optimal outcomes, which is the theoretical underpinning of global and regional trade liberalisation. In his view, instead of a blanket approach to trade liberalisation, there should be selectivity and sequencing of the process, complemented by strategies to build up technological and managerial capabilities among producers at the micro-level, and to empower the poor and the marginalised. According to Girvan, 'universalistic neo-liberalism' should be replaced by diversity and acceptance of the principles of pluralism, particularity and learning. Counter-globalisation therefore questions the theory, the ideology, and the policies of neo-liberal globalisation.

In reflecting upon the impact of the international financial crisis, Girvan believes that the growing consensus among mainstream economists on the need for government regulation of financial systems and, more generally, of the market economy as a whole, provides a window of opportunity for the developing countries to formulate a counter strategy to the current approach to globalisation. He argues, however, that the increasing heterogeneity among the countries of the South would necessitate new approaches and innovative strategies for reconciling differences within the Group of 77. In this context, he feels that the Caribbean countries would need to review their position within the overall setting of the South and the broad currents of the counter-globalisation movement. From a strategic perspective, Girvan suggests that an effective response by the Caribbean countries to the challenges posed by globalisation should be based on a strategy of 'walking on two legs', which involves the strengthening of the bargaining position and negotiating capacity of the states in the region in their external relations. It also requires a strengthening of the productive capacity of regional producers to participate successfully in markets that are increasingly hemispheric and global in scope. Moreover, he argues that the Caribbean, together with other regions in the South, should challenge the principle of 'universalistic neo-liberalism' on which current international trade and economic negotiations are based.

In his contribution entitled 'Globalisation and Small Developing Countries: The Imperative for Repositioning', Richard Bernal sees globalisation as a multi-dimensional process which encompasses economic, political, technological, social, cultural and psychological factors. In this context, he sees the small developing countries as particularly exposed to the effects of globalisation. He identifies several disadvantages faced by these countries in terms of their dependence on a limited range of commodity exports, high trading ratios, diseconomies of scale and structural vulnerabilities. Bernal believes, nevertheless, that these countries could reduce the adverse implications of globalisation and take advantage of opportunities offered by the process on the basis of a strategy of 'global repositioning'. He feels that the extent to which these countries could seize the opportunities offered by globalisation will depend on the implementation of a comprehensive process of structural transformation, not merely structural adjustment. In advocating a policy of strategic global repositioning, Bernal states that such a policy should be based on the consolidation and improvement of existing production structures and the reorientation of the economy based on the creation of new types of economic activities. It would also require policies aimed at improving the competitiveness and efficiency of enterprises by stimulating the creation of an entrepreneurial environment. In addition, the strategy should be based on selective trade, fiscal and credit policies supported by medium-term education and technology policies focused on strategic sectors as well as on close co-operation between government and the private sector. He believes that the capacity of small countries to capitalise on the opportunities offered by globalisation would also depend on the adoption of a stable macroeconomic policy framework conducive to the encouragement of investment. It should also include a policy of diversification of exports. Bernal believes, however, that the small economies would also need to focus on the services sector, which represents the fastest growing sector in the global economy, instead of manufacturing, which he feels has lost its dynamism. In this regard, he feels that small economies should be innovative in pursuing the establishment of new industries based on strategic corporate alliances and the modernisation of international marketing techniques. At the same time, Bernal believes that, at the international level, the existence of disparities in size must be addressed by ensuring that international regulatory regimes and institutions take account of the needs of the small economies. In other words, the international community must mediate the encounter between small countries and their larger counterparts in the global market place.

In the paper on 'Globalisation and Regional Economic Integration', Byron Blake points to two potentially contradictory and overlapping trends, namely, globalisation and regionalisation, which have dominated international economic relations during the last decade of the twentieth century. Against this background, Blake describes the evolution of regional integration and also the philosophical assumptions and institutional arrangements underpinning globalisation centred on the Uruguay Round agreements. He goes on to argue that globalisation has undermined some of the objectives of regional economic integration, most notably in terms of the granting of certain advantages to member states and the opportunity to obtain non-reciprocal trade advantages in the markets of the developed countries which are not available to third countries. Moreover, the tendency to form integration and cooperation arrangements embracing both developed and developing countries has also served to undermine the traditional integration arrangements involving only developing countries.

In her article, the 'Impact of Globalisation on the Caribbean', Jessica Byron's analysis makes special reference to the experience of small states of the Eastern Caribbean. Following Scholte, she acknowledges that globalisation has introduced qualitative changes in the organisation and capabilities of the nation state. Moreover, she sees globalisation as producing new manifestations of marginalisation and inequality. In the specific circumstances of the Caribbean, she points to the fact that, in spite of the continuing structural vulnerability of the small economies of the region, the advent of globalisation has led to the reduction in the level of preferences previously enjoyed by these countries, a decline in their export earnings as well as financial flows. According to Byron, as a result of these developments, the OECS countries have experienced growing vulnerability to external factors. Consequently, there is an urgent need to strengthen their competitiveness in the global economy and also to capitalise on their proximity to the US market, in order to avoid marginalisation in the global economy. However, the disruption in the marketing of bananas in the European Union, caused by the challenge to the traditional preferential arrangements enjoyed by the OECS countries and the WTO ruling on the subject, could lead to social and political upheaval. Byron states that, in confronting the challenges facing them, the small states of the region should seek to reapportion administrative, technical and management functions among national, regional and other sectors. In addition, the state should play a proactive role in promoting human resources development, infrastructure development and in cushioning the social impact of adjustment in order to prevent social disintegration. At the international level, Byron asserts that it will be necessary for the Caribbean microstates to radically rethink their diplomatic strategies and their international relations, in terms of improved training for foreign service personnel and their strategic location, to deal with issues such as those discussed within the WTO. Moreover, given the prospect of the creation of a western hemispheric free trade arrangement (FTAA), increased resources would need to be allocated to strengthen diplomatic and commercial representations. These countries would also need to identify opportunities for promoting South-South solidarity and co-operation.

Finally, Charles Ross, in his paper entitled 'Globalisation and the Private Sector', unapologetically embraces a private sector perspective in pointing to the opportunities offered by globalisation. He sees great possibilities for combining the capital and technology of the North with the labour and natural resources of the South in order to increase output, employment, and overall living standards in the developing countries. He points to the increased openness of markets in the developed countries as an important feature of globalisation, which provides market access for exports from the developing countries. As he sees it, the challenge facing the developing countries is to organise their economies in such a way as to make them attractive for investment geared to the production of internationally competitive goods and services. However, in his view, the creation of such an environment in the developing countries would require the adoption of policies which do not distort prices and resource allocation in the economy, while at the same time encouraging domestic earnings and investment instead of consumption. He concedes that globalisation does harbour some dangers for the developing countries, but he feels that the developing countries should make a conscious effort to take advantage of the opportunities offered by globalisation. He also feels that the encouragement of foreign direct investment is the most constructive way of achieving this objective. However, Ross does not believe that the developing countries should continue to base their development on preferential access for their commodities to traditional markets in Europe and North America, but that they should instead seek to engage in reciprocal trade. Consequently, they should focus on the production of tradable goods and services on an internationally competitive basis. Indeed, Ross sees the increase in the rate of economic growth in the developing countries as the most sustainable way of achieving poverty reduction. He recognises the need, nevertheless, to ensure that capital entering the developing countries is used for investment in the productive sector and that as little as possible enters as short-term speculative capital.

It is clear that the papers presented in this volume reflect a number of different philosophical and ideological perspectives on globalisation and economic liberalisation and the type of strategic responses that should be adopted by the developing countries in seeking to deal with the challenges posed by them. For example, while Bernal and Ross tend to support a private sector-led, market-oriented approach to development as a response to the challenges posed by globalisation, Girvan and Thomas argue in favour of a managed approach to economic policy, based on a more balanced relationship between the state and the private sector. Moreover, in contrast to Bernal and Ross, who embrace, to varying degrees, elements of a neo-liberal policy stance, Girvan and Thomas subscribe to a structuralist/institutionalist approach which recognises the need to take account of the specific circumstances of the countries involved, in grappling with the problem of globalisation. Further, whereas the former are prepared to abandon the traditional preferential arrangements enjoyed by the developing countries, the latter see the retention of such preferences as a necessary part of a rational multilateral trading system. However, they all acknowledge, in one way or another, the need for the international community to extend some concessions to the smaller economies in order to enable them to function effectively in the global economy. Moreover, the majority of the contributors recognise the need for the developing countries to seek to recapture the intellectual initiative in order to ensure the formulation of a strategy designed to make globalisation more consistent with their development needs and priorities.

These differences notwithstanding, all of the essays are written from the perspective of the developing countries and should therefore enrich the ongoing debate on the merits and demerits of globalisation. Even more important, however, is the fact that the articles in the volume offer important insights which could contribute to the formulation of alternative approaches to globalisation, consistent with the establishment of an enlightened global order in which economic benefits are more evenly distributed among all countries.

1

Intellectual Hegemony in the Context of Globalisation

BRANISLAV GOSOVIC

The Importance of 'Intellectual Hegemony'

An examination of the subject of the intellectual hegemony imposed by the North is of vital importance because one of the key aspects of globalisation is its increasing standardisation and uniformity in thinking regarding the world economic system, the development process, and the prescriptions and strategies for action.

'Intellectual hegemony', which is projected on a global scale, is inherently undemocratic and totalitarian in nature, and has become a major tool in the hands of those with political, economic, military and communications power. It is a powerful instrument for global domination, and it is used to shape and control the outlook and thinking of policy makers, as well as public opinion, regarding contemporary social, economic and political phenomena. It is a means of discouraging and, indeed, preventing, meaningful dissent or alternative thinking, which could challenge or engender doubts about the prevailing order and the systemic relationships which underpin it. Its ideological content, hailed as 'consensus', is underpinned by specific theoretical assumptions and is inspired by a set of geopolitical strategies and interests. It has been foisted unilaterally on the world community without allowing an opportunity for democratic debate or participation in the process, and under threat that countries which do not subscribe to globalisation will be isolated and left behind by this 'speeding locomotive' with no chance of enjoying the fruits of the promising new era of prosperity being embarked upon.

The current intellectual dominance of the developed countries is of special significance to the developing countries, acting individually and collectively, as they attempt to confront and manage the challenges posed by globalisation, which has been defined and driven almost exclusively by a small number of players from the North, in pursuit of their interests and in keeping with their vision of a new world order. It has created an 'intellectual dependency' of the countries of the South for data, analysis, policy and prescriptions, and is thus a major ingredient in eroding their sovereignty. It has had the effect of delegitimising major elements of the development agenda, and of marginalising the concerns of the developing countries. In fact, it has sought to negate the basic arguments and premises which underpin their national and international development efforts, since these cannot be accommodated within the now dominant paradigm which, in the context of a globally imposed uniformity and hegemony, cannot easily be challenged. Indeed, any challenge or critique of the prevailing orthodoxy or the proposal of alternatives, is regarded as heretical and is simply ridiculed, dismissed or ignored.

The prevailing ideological orthodoxy has had an insidious impact on, and has significantly eroded multilateralism, which is the foundation and, indeed, the inspiration of international organisations. It has played a key role in changing the nature, outlook, and work of the United Nations, and of international organisations in general, increasingly turning them into instruments controlled by powerful countries and interests, thus weakening their democratic character and intent.

The establishment of a hegemonic intellectual culture is one of the principal tools used by the North to dismantle and neutralise political and intellectual challenges from the South, in terms of collective action, in the field of development. By the same token, it has served as a major instrument for influencing and shaping national political and economic strategies, and for controlling the initiatives taken by the South in the economic, political, social and cultural spheres. Although 'intellectual hegemony' is one of the linchpins of the new North-dominated world order, it is often not perceived as such. Indeed, all too frequently it is accepted with enthusiasm even in some parts of the developing world. Even when it is perceived as oppressive, many people simply give up in despair, in the belief that it cannot be challenged or resisted, while others, regarding their position as 'realistic', accept it as a fact of life.

Ideological hegemony is an issue that needs to be fully recognised and tackled as a top priority in any attempt to affect the content and direction of the existing global order and of international co-operation, as it is currently practised, in order to make them democratic, development-oriented and more responsive to, and supportive of, development needs.

Mechanisms used for Projecting and Maintaining Global Intellectual Hegemony

Global intellectual hegemony is projected systematically and is buttressed by a number of instruments, perfected at the national level, but now applied on a worldwide basis. This development has been made possible and facilitated by new technologies and modes of communication, and by the control of these instruments by the forces favouring and promoting the currently dominant paradigm.

A great deal is achieved by the skilful use of words and terminology, both to rationalise the current order and endow it with positive qualities. At the same time, a concerted effort is made to belittle or demonise any challenge mounted against it. Consequently, the current globalising world order is labelled as a 'new' and irresistible tide of history, and is therefore viewed positively. Any question or issue raised from a development perspective is dismissed as belonging to the past and as a remnant of the NIEO, which is viewed as anathema in the currently dominant iconography. The application of this label is used as an effective way of forestalling argument and debate. Moreover, the fear of being labelled in this manner has in turn played a major role in encouraging defensiveness on the part of the spokesmen and leaders of the developing countries.

Terms such as the 'end of ideology', 'end of conflict', 'partnership', 'stakeholders', 'opportunity', and 'no more South or North' are frequently used in contemporary international development discourse. They are meant to pre-empt questions that may be asked about the soundness of the system, and whether the countries of the South are getting an optimal deal or whether their interests are as well served by the system as those of the North.

Co-optation of words and terminology from the UN development vocabulary has been used to neutralise the political and intellectual challenge from the South and to move the discussion on international development issues to those institutions which are under the control of the countries of the North, a factor which has not only made possible the control of the process, but has also endowed these institutions, which have become the dominant source of analysis and prescription, with added legitimacy in the eyes of the South.

Words and labels have also been employed as a technique to dismiss and delegitimise awkward questions and arguments, and often to demonise those who raise issues which are legitimate and valid, and which indeed have been an essential feature of the work of the United Nations for decades. A number of terms such as equity, self-reliance and exploitation are now frowned upon and have virtually disappeared from international discourse. At the same time, new concepts, such as 'level playing field', are propagated by the developed countries which, in a highly unequal world and given varying levels of development, are prejudicial to the national development objectives and the sovereignty of developing countries.

Fear and intimidation play a significant role in the lack of challenge to the current intellectual hegemony. Governments do not speak up for fear of retaliation. Individuals, especially those in the service of governments and international organisations, have been reluctant to speak frankly on issues, which unfortunately projects a mistaken image of harmony and consensus. This phenomenon has been well illustrated by what could be called the 'Stiglitz syndrome'. The critique of the Washington Consensus by Joseph Stiglitz, the former chief economist of the World Bank, was seen as a signal from the top, emboldening many to begin to question and criticise 'globalisation', of which only a short time before they were singing praises.

Indeed, what is taking place is tantamount to a process of global brain-washing, which is made possible by modern technology and by the concentration of control over the global media, mainly by the North. The increasing dependence of the world public for information and knowledge on simple messages, mostly from TV, and reflecting the same intellectual orientation, has contributed to the development of herd-like behaviour and reactions in many quarters. The discontinuity with the development and de-colonisation past, the de-legitimisation of UN development work and the traditional North-South agenda, which are part and parcel of the current intellectual hegemony, have resulted in significant disorientation among the developing countries.

The Weak Links in Responding to the Current Intellectual Hegemony: The South and the United Nations

A major factor contributing to the current intellectual hegemony has been the lack of a serious intellectual challenge in the face of the de facto intellectual disarmament of the South. This has been combined with the weakening of the United Nations as a source of autonomous thinking and analysis, inspired by the development objectives and the basic premises of the UN Charter, which entrusted the organisation with a mandate for promoting development.

Regarding the posture of the developing countries, their impact and influence on the global system and on the dominant paradigm waned as their collective action weakened. Moreover, while the developing countries could agree on those aspects of the new ideology to which they were opposed, this by itself was not enough to counter effectively the new dispensation or to present an alternative platform of proposals. This was in part due to the erosion of the role of the UN on which the developing countries relied, in an earlier period, for intellectual, technical and policy support.

Indeed, up to the early 1980s the UN had played an important role in mounting the intellectual challenge to the traditional North-dominated international economic system. This was most prominently reflected in the creation of UNCTAD, based on the precedent and experience of ECLAC. The creation of UNCTAD was instrumental in the birth of G77 and in its success and ability to confront and negotiate with the North. It is not surprising that one of the main objectives of the proponents of the emerging intellectual hegemony is to limit and neutralise the role of the UN and thus remove an important intellectual support to the developing countries which could act as a political force in challenging the system. This objective was achieved in a number of different ways, including: the imposition of limits on budget and on personnel as well as restrictions on mandate, especially in the economic sphere; emasculation of the traditional development agenda and its reorientation towards issues of special concern to the North, including human rights (all of which are designed to put the developing countries on the defensive); the application of pressure on selected UN organisations and, in particular, efforts to abolish UNCTAD, UNIDO and ECLAC – three organisations which were specially identified with providing support for the South and with the promotion of a development agenda; and the promotion of the multilateral financial institutions, and of the WTO, as instruments not only for steering the world economy and articulating the intellectual underpinnings of the current paradigm, but also for actively influencing economic policy in the developing countries through multiple forms of conditionalities, an externally imposed adjustment process, and the exclusion of a number of critical issues from research and debate.

Strategies for Challenging the Global Intellectual Hegemony

The first and most important step in mounting a challenge to the current North-based intellectual hegemony is to develop an awareness of its existence, and also an understanding of its importance and impact on the South. Such awareness and understanding of the hegemony of ideas and the dominance of the theoretical constructs based on Northern interests are required in policy-making circles, in the media, the general public and, most of all, in the academic and intellectual communities of the South, which will need to work out responses to the current situation on the basis of the articulation of an alternative development paradigm consistent with the needs and interests of the South.

Another essential step in this direction is to identify the overarching interests that unite the developing countries in their effort to change the dominant system, to promote their national development objectives, and defend their political and economic sovereignty. It will also be necessary to identify the similarities and differences in national situations and the challenges facing the developing countries, since it is on the basis of such an understanding that the developing countries will be able to build a collective stand regarding the global structures, regimes and, indeed, the intellectual paradigms that underpin them.

In practical terms, this calls for the strengthening of the intellectual capacities of the South by combining analysis and research and ultimately distilling and formulating a South strategy on the major challenges facing the international community and, in particular, the United Nations as a democratic instrument for the promotion of multilateralism.

In other words, the organisation and the promotion of structured relations and links between the countries of the South are urgently required. Fortunately, at the South Summit held in Havana, Cuba in April 2000 the developing countries were able to begin the process of challenging the intellectual hegemony of the North and to structure responses which are strategically important in orienting the global system as well as national policies. In this context, a concerted effort will also need to be made to strengthen the UN as the global leader in policy formulation and research in order to enable it to act in accordance with its Charter in promoting the global objectives of democracy and development, which have been embedded in its work over the past five decades.

The efforts within the South and within the UN to cope with the challenges of a North-driven intellectual hegemony would need to be linked with those of sympathetic intellectual and academic circles in the North. The forging of such a coalition of forces is essential in mounting a successful challenge to the hegemony of ideas and the theoretical constructs that have been foisted upon the international community in the wake of the power vacuum that arose at the end of the Cold War and the subsequent emergence of a uni-polar geopolitical order. Such an initiative is also important in promoting freedom of thought and expression, as a prerequisite for the creation of a truly democratic international community and a global political and economic environment which fosters development in the interests of all countries and not only those in the North.

2

Globalisation as Paradigm Shift

Response from the South

CLIVE THOMAS

Introduction

Recent events suggest that we are at a crucial watershed in the evolution of the global economy. Over the past decade we have witnessed repeated financial crises. We are in the midst of an extended crisis in the major emerging financial markets and economies, a growing inequality and unevenness in global output and consumption, severe difficulties in managing the post-WTO architecture of international trade and investment, and an intense conflict of ideas about the roles of the state, private business and 'civil society' in the formulation of national, regional, and international policies. All these concerns are framed in the context of globalisation. It is significant that we live in a region whose modern history, perhaps more than any other, was shaped by the evolution of the global economy. The Caribbean was the nursery in which many of the original elements of global capitalism and the world market were nurtured. Indeed, the plantation, which came to dominate Caribbean societies, is in many respects a prototype of the most characteristic institution of globalisation – the modern TNC. This paper offers an interpretation of globalisation, and on this basis, sketches the outline of a response from the South.

Paradigm Shift

Because the region's development is so closely associated with the evolution of global markets for goods, services, productive factors and financial assets, the temptation for Caribbean analysts is to stress historical continuities in the present global situation. Many are understandingly, but mistakenly, skeptical of the newness or modernity of globalisation. They point out that the present scale of human migration, which is considered to be exceptional, resulting in one in every 100 persons living outside the country of their birth, pales into insignificance when compared to the historical movement of Caribbean populations. Despite the leading role attributed to TNC international production in globalisation, domestic markets still absorb more than 80 per cent of global output and over 90 per cent of employees worldwide service domestic markets. In general also, the efficiency, capacity, dynamism, and competitiveness of TNCs in the global economy cannot be distinguished from their national origins.

International trade as a proportion of GDP is not significantly greater today (14 per cent for the industrialised countries) than it was in 1913 (13 per cent). The same holds true for foreign investment. The direct investment/GDP ratio of the developed economies is the same today (4 per cent), as it was in 1913, and less than the 1890s. It is estimated that over 90 per cent of global fixed capital formation is financed from domestic savings. Rough estimates of global capital stock of US$60,000 billion in 1997 (estimated at twice global production of US$30,000 billion) indicate that the accumulated value of foreign investment by TNCs of $3,500 billion represents six per cent of the total, and this rate is the same as it was a century ago. Moreover, globalisation of short-term capital flows, which are nearly 24 times as large as long-term investments, dominates capital markets.

Compared with today, the role of science and technology in earlier periods of overseas expansion in the Caribbean was also profound and covered simultaneously many fields of human endeavour: health, nutrition, weaponry, navigation, agriculture, finance, institutional development, clothing and manufactured items. Despite their pronounced international character, the 'foreign' representation on the Boards of Directors of TNCs is still very token, and most of their employees, assets, investors, and Research and Development (R&D) remain in the home country. The resolute pursuit of liberalisation today was matched in earlier epochs, particularly in the period of colonial expansion. Indeed, historically there were lower tariff and non-tariff barriers to trade, and fewer restrictions on investment flows between the region and its various metropoles, than is the case today. Much as it is today, during colonial times regionalisation was also a major issue. Imperial blocs, currency zones (sterling, French franc) the US Monroe Doctrine, and attempts at selective regional integration of the Caribbean, all preceded the regionalisation associated with contemporary globalisation.

The list can go on. While there is truth to each of these observations, I have argued elsewhere that, in light of the empirical material I have unearthed for a forthcoming study, the world as a whole is experiencing an unprecedented transformation. Change is manifest at an exceptional pace in a highly compressed period of time and in a truly multi-dimensional way. It affects all areas of human experience: material and non-material, economic as well as political, social, cultural, institutional, and environmental. Some examples of these are:

- Unprecedented changes in ideas, belief systems (social construction), politics and ideology, at both the global and national level
- A transformed international system. This is evident in the collapse of the previous bipolar world and its two rival ideologies; the resultant disappearance of important 'third spaces' previously exploited by developing countries; the emergence of a single hegemonic power and ideology; the break-up of old states; the emergence of new ones; and dramatic changes in global forms of inter-governmental management
- A growing proliferation of social problems, many of which are 'transboundary' and global in scope. For example, the rapid growth of migratory populations and its wide ranging consequences; narco-trafficking and money laundering; violence and terrorism; unemployment and growth without jobs; social and cultural homogenisation and exclusion; war, and civil conflict
- The unprecedented rise of global forms of inter-governmental management. This has led to the emergence of sites of authority and legislative power that cover areas which hitherto were seen as falling within the compass of states and, indeed, as defining their sovereign role in the international community, e.g. the regulation of capital flows and macroeconomic policies
- An unprecedented intensification of environmental threats to the sustainability of planet earth

Most commentators also believe that the present scientific and technical revolution is truly unprecedented, particularly in areas that promote market integration – communications, transport, information and weaponry (enforcement). It has been estimated that over 95 per cent of all scientists and technologists who ever lived are alive today (P. Kennedy, 1998). The commercialisation of knowledge and the rise of the consultancy industry in what is termed the 'new mode of intellectual authority' underscore the qualitative shift in the roles of science and technology in society.

There are also examples of great changes in the global economy. Thus we find:

- Exceptional growth of international production led by TNCs. This now occurs at a faster rate than either the growth of global trade or GDP
- Despite the grave difficulties of measuring global FDI flows and the numerous inaccuracies and internal inconsistencies found in the published data (see R. Sutcliffe, 1998), it is clear that private foreign investment is growing spectacularly, even though this is concentrated in a few economies and among a few firms, and is facilitated by the growth of cross-border mergers and acquisitions, inter-firm agreements, the worldwide introduction of liberalised private FDI regimes, and the recent wave of privatisations
- Current global consumption has doubled since the mid 1970s. Consumer markets are integrated worldwide to a point where some fear a global monoculture
- Financial capital plays a leading role in globalisation. Growth in the volume and speculative character of global financial flows, particularly highly leveraged hedge funds, has introduced a striking divorce between the traditional bond of the performance of a country's currency and the performance of its 'economic fundamentals'
- There is rapid growth in regionalisation and the formation of megablocks. This is associated with the erosion of one-way preferences and non-reciprocity for the exports of developing economies, as well as a remarkable decline in the real prices of commodities traded internationally
- Although racial, cultural and other barriers to the free movement of labour remain, a fundamental transformation and basic reconfiguration of labour markets worldwide is nevertheless underway
- Far-reaching corporate re-organisation and changes in the structure of firm competition are very evident. The growth of TNCs is the best demonstration of this trend. This relates to the increased role played by 'captive exchanges' in international trade and the reduced significance of geography and national territory in defining the mobility of firm assets
- The modalities of contemporary liberalisation are also unique. There is now a concentration of power and authority over the process that mirrors

global economic concentration. National governments have lost, in varying degrees, control over their domestic economic affairs
- Entrepreneurial perception has shifted dramatically. Recent interviews
conducted by UNCTAD with 300 TNC managers indicate that over
one-half view their companies as fully global and highly coordinated
internationally. This has increased from one-third in 1990. Eighty per
cent projected that this would be the position of their firm by 2002
- Uneven growth and development accompany these economic manifestations. The major global economic performance indicators – output,
consumption, trade, investment, and prices – reveal this state of affairs.

The varying impacts of these outcomes on countries, individuals, and
groups indicate that a truly fundamental process is at work. This process,
however, is driven by human activity in a variety of forms. The intuitive
conclusion I draw from this is that the process has produced an unmistak-
able paradigm shift, both in the way in which the world is conceived and
how it is acted upon (C.Y. Thomas, 1998 A). While a borderless world is far
from a reality, in recent times the inter-regional and international scope of
many forms of social, political, economic, and cultural activities has dramatically intensified and broadened. The dynamic interconnectedness of
contemporary global society is far more extensive and intensive than it has
ever been, and seems destined to continue this way. Far more than any
previous era, human endeavours are conceived, designed and implemented
as global projects. Whether it is the activities of powerful TNCs, the actions
of billions of individual consumers or citizens worldwide, the pursuit of
national defence and national interests, the promotion of culture and a
sense of community at the local or national levels, the provision of health
care, the advocacy of social and environmental concerns, the injunction
'Think globally' is followed more and more every day. This, I believe, is the
most decisive feature of our age.

Globalisation and Liberalisation

Political commitment to policies of liberalisation is a major force driving
global change. To that extent, globalisation and liberalisation are often, but
inaccurately, identified as mirror images of the same process. This confla-
tion of two separate processes, however, is contrived and not a necessary
condition. As the UNDP states:

> A dominant economic theme of the 1990s, globalisation encapsulates both a
> description and a prescription. The description is the widening and deepening
> of international flows of trade, finance and information in a single, integrated

global market. The prescription is to liberalize national and global markets in the belief that free flows of trade, finance and information will produce the best outcome for growth and human welfare. All is presented with an air of inevitability and overwhelming conviction. Not since the heyday of free trade in the 19th century has economic theory elicited such widespread certainty. (UNDP, 1997 p.82)

While the description of globalisation is overly economistic and the interpretation of the prescription is very close to the mark, it is very dangerous to collapse globalisation and liberalisation into a single process. Many familiar political and ideological circumstances propel the expansion of neo-liberal policies in the South and encourage this view: the proliferation of externally designed and financed SAPs; the external indebtedness and reliance of many countries on external debt relief and/or support from international financial institutions; political changes within the developed countries, which impact on their operations in the international economy; and the break-up of the bipolar world and the disappearance of 'third spaces' for alternative political and economic policies to which reference was previously made. The result is that the inexorable movement in the direction of globalisation represents itself as an inevitable political option for neo-liberal policies.

Although politically and ideologically driven, this development is rationalised in economic terms. The argument is that globalisation carries the economic benefits of specialisation and the division of labour to the world level. Liberalisation, a process that promotes competitiveness, permits the reaping of economies of scale, secures economic restructuring and industrial re-organisation, provides for the wider availability of technology, and offers dynamic opportunities and gains for far-sighted, risk-taking entrepreneurs, is inseparable from it. Therefore all policies which directly or indirectly remove barriers and impediments to market expansion contribute to global economic growth and promote human welfare worldwide.

The premise of this argument is that markets uniformly promote competition and efficiency. They are socially cohesive institutions in that they form the meeting place for the mutually shared interests of producers and consumers. Consequently, free world markets for commodities, services, productive factors, and finance would secure the global convergence of economic and political systems and an end to conflict between nations, ideologies, and systems. Further, if development means expanding options and opportunities, as it has come to be accepted, then unfettered globalisation – that is, liberalisation – assures these outcomes.

An important corollary to this argument is that a 'minimalist' state facilitates globalisation, which focuses on market support, regulatory activities, and the provision of maximum opportunities for private individuals and firms to own, control, and distribute society's resources. At the global level, inter-state organisations work within rule-based agreements, which permit little or no discretionary authority, but which nevertheless carry built-in mechanisms of enforcement to ensure compliance.

This approach glibly overlooks the instabilities and inequalities in rates of growth and economic performance, frequently associated with markets left to their own devices. In this period of accelerated globalisation, markets have widened gaps in income, wealth, consumption, power, capabilities, and access, both among countries and within them.[1] This is not a single unfortunate outcome, but part of a repeated global record. By definition, markets respond to money income, not just needs. Consequently, instead of being universally socially cohesive, they lay stress on the survival of the fittest, the private, the personal, and the individual. The likelihood therefore is that unrestrained market-led development can be destabilising, conflictual, and contradictory. It has potentially lethal self-destructive properties, since its very 'successes' can breed polarisation, which in turn produces conflicts and challenges to the process itself. Therefore, if globalisation remains an exclusively market-driven process, rather than leading to the eventual inclusion and integration of countries and groups within countries, as it is hoped, it may well continue to produce the opposite: exclusion, disintegration, and marginalisation, because of the uneven distribution of its benefits and costs.

It is incorrect to treat global markets as benign mechanisms that simply produce price signals to guide resource allocation. As social institutions, they necessarily embrace certain properties, and power is one of these. But, while power is vested in global markets, their effectiveness depends on a conglomeration of other social attributes: trust, rules, rights and obligations, informational access, the regulation of participants, and the certainty of enforcement. It is also dependent on a conglomeration of economic circumstances, which do not always obtain. Thus, asymmetric information flows, monopoly, bounded rationality, scale economies, as well as deceit, fraud, corruption, and other such illegalities undermine market structures. These considerations are not novel. They have long been recognised in economic theory and have provided justification for institutional intervention to prevent the occurrence of market deformations. Consider, for example, the anti-monopoly interventions in developed market economies. Rather, therefore, than a doctrinaire appeal to a minimalist state as a facilitator of globalisation, the process may be better served by the collective political and social action of states and international organisations, explicitly designed to secure beneficial outcomes. Put bluntly, political and social determination of the operational framework of global markets is a necessary condition for successful globalisation.

In many of the debates, these issues are polarised. They are presented as a sharp dichotomy: either extreme *laissez-faire* or extensive state ownership and intervention in the economy. In real life, however, choices never emerge in this stark manner. There is a wide spectrum of multicultural capitalism; ranging from US libertarian capitalism through different brands of West European welfare capitalism and Japanese capitalism, to the enormous variations of capitalist societies found in the developing countries of Latin America, Asia, Africa, and the Caribbean.

In concluding these comments on the links between globalisation and liberalisation, it is noteworthy that the mechanisms of liberalisation are as uneven as the outcomes of global growth. While agencies like the IMF, World Bank, and the WTO have tremendous roles, more democratic organisations like the United Nations have seen their roles diminished in economic and social matters.

Response from the South

The shift from a conceptual pre-occupation with the national to the global, linked to a global process that brings cultures into irreversible contact with one another, is of incalculable importance to all states, and particularly to the South. A consequence of this paradigm shift is that any dialogue, debate, analysis or policy position taken at the national, regional or global level, which fails to embrace this reality will be ignored and made ineffective. In such circumstances, it is preferable to stress the disjuncture with the past that globalisation represents, rather than the continuities of historical experience, important as these undoubtedly are. The contribution that critique and deconstruction provide to the de-mystification of the political and ideological trappings attached to globalisation, is also important. Contending world views and struggles over the hegemony of ideas about development are an important part of the global project of the South. So too is the need to advance constructive options, from which programmatic formulations for a way forward might be forged. In other words, critical thought must lead to purposeful social and political action. The final section of this paper addresses these issues from the standpoint of economic concerns.

Although neo-liberalism/the 'Washington Consensus' is frequently presented as a monolithic and universal view, which yields one scientific economic methodology and one logical and, therefore, valid set of policy instruments to go with it and yet although at present globalisation is driven by private business interests, either acting on their own or through governments and inter-governmental bodies, there are significant opportunities in the South for public, private, and civil society interventions to secure an equitable distribution of the costs and production gains of a globalised approach to economic activities. This observation is not surprising. From its inception, several routes to the insertion of national economies into the world market have existed. The record shows that routes taken depend on national patterns of political and social change, and technological development and capital accumulation, in response to the prevailing pattern of global expansion of capitalist firms in the world market. The recent crisis of emerging markets in Asia and Latin America has already led to significant shifts in public policy in this regard. Capital controls that protect against highly leveraged international hedge funds have reappeared. Financial repression, aimed at containing the contagion effects of disruptions elsewhere, has been reintroduced in some countries. In some cases previously privatised ventures have been reacquired by governments. Citizens have rebelled against the moral hazard of using the public purse to benefit those financial institutions that have taken imprudent risks with their depositors' money. There are many and varied calls for prudential and regulatory oversight of global financial institutions, as well as for taxes on hot money flows. Furthermore, TNCs invest highly in China, although it is the least 'open' of the developing countries.

The scope for the effective pursuit of existing options is, however, dependent on the domestic platform on which the economy is based. In the present age of already significantly globalised economic activity, the strength of that platform in the South is dependent on the following:

- The state of domestic economic reform, particularly in regard to wide access for the population to productive assets, credit, finance, knowledge and training; the regeneration of economic institutions; the extent of social cohesion; and the existence of a broad-based national consensus on national priorities
- Macroeconomic stability, and in particular the purposive and effective exercise of monetary and fiscal policies
- A firm national commitment to an anti-poverty agenda and people-focused development
- The ongoing restructuring of political and social institutions

- The resolute promotion of solidarity with other developing countries in the region in which the country is located, and with the wider South.

There is no 'one size fits all' approach to the patterns of domestic reform. The South itself is an increasingly differentiated group of countries. What can be said in confidence, however, is that in the absence of a strong domestic platform, developing countries have no option but to comply with the conditionalities that accompany externally financed SAPs and debt-reduction programmes. As we know, these are premised on the neo-liberal/'Washington Consensus' approach to national and international development.

While domestic reform is crucial, the interface between domestic reform and a progressive external response from the South is also important for positive outcomes from globalisation. What then should guide this external response? Briefly, there are three general but interactive foci around which the South's response in international economic bodies and fora, might profitably be organised. First, there is the global focus. There are many fundamental global issues, both new and long-standing, in which the South has a vital interest. Among the new ones are: monitoring and surveillance of the global economy; post-WTO developments in trade and related matters; and global environmental issues. There are the issues long advocated by the South, which remain crucial to the creation of a supportive international environment for development and which have all but disappeared from the global agenda. These include the adjustment mechanism for capital deficient and foreign-exchange-poor developing countries; commodity markets; development finance; market access for exports from the South; knowledge, training, and technological transfer; and international poverty alleviation.

Unfortunately, the success of neo-liberalism has led to the de-legitimisation of the South as a purposeful category in almost all the developed economies. This has undermined their collective actions and dissipated the earlier moral gains that came from the wide acceptance of the idea of international responsibility for deliberate state action by all countries to construct an institutional framework supportive of development, based on recognition of the principle that the 'playing field' in global markets is far from level. In response to this critical state of affairs, two priority thrusts suggest themselves for the South:

- Support for the UN generally, and in particular the extension of its influence over global, social, and economic affairs. The basis of this proposal is the more representative nature of the UN as compared to the present dominant institutions: the IMF, World Bank, and WTO

– Complementing this proposal is, the advocacy of reform of these institutions – supported by technical studies. Such reform should be consistent with the broader objectives to democratise their operations and to make them more responsive and oriented to the development priorities of the South.

The second focus is South-South co-operation. Although a number of South institutions promote this type of co-operation, including the South Centre, Non-Aligned Movement (NAM), the G15, the G77 and China, the South remains distressingly under-equipped, under-financed, under-staffed and under-institutionalised for the tasks that confront it. While resources are limited, this alone cannot explain the vast disproportion in resources between such agencies as the OECD and its equivalent in the South. As the Chairman of the South Centre remarked at the second Meeting of the Council of Representatives of the Centre (September 1997, New York), the OECD has a staff of 2,000 and a budget in excess of $330 million. The South Centre, after years of effort, still cannot raise the capital endowment of $30 million which it requires from member countries. Surely a clear priority is to redress this woeful state of affairs. One hopes that the South would address this matter of institutionalisation urgently and definitively.

There are other immediate issues related to South-South co-operation. One is the creation of modalities through which the interests of the South as a group can be represented at the highest level. A number of tasks require this representation in international fora, including focusing on global economic surveillance and management, to which reference has been made. These include resolving the contradictions which arise from mega-blocks that include both developed and developing countries within them. This often runs the risk of erosion of general preferences for all developing countries and discrimination against developing countries that are not members. Yet another is the need to ensure that bodies like the G77 and China add real value beyond other gatherings in which countries and groups of countries in the South participate.

The third focus is on regional, sub-regional, and even bilateral groupings of countries from the South. This is a process that has been actively underway for sometime now and has produced a large number of such co-operative arrangements. What seems to be lacking is the explicit development of this process in a manner complementary to the two other foci.

There are additional issue areas that fall within these three foci. These include:

- Implementation of the Agenda 21 package of environmental and sustainable development measures and agreements
- Reform of the global financial architecture so as to minimise exposure to disruptions caused by short-term speculative flows of highly leveraged funds; to ensure accountability, transparency, and adequate disclosure; to provide supervision and prudential oversight of global finance houses; and to secure a balance between the interests of creditors and debtors.[2]
- Joint development of science and technology
- Joint activity in areas such as space exploration, environment, and information sharing (e.g. health and epidemiological data, disaster preparedness and crime)
- The promotion of common social standards, such as the ratification and enforcement of existing ILO conventions.

Conclusion

The great danger faced by the South is that globalisation, which is here to stay, is accepted as the exclusive product of liberalisation and the market economy. If this occurs, the market will come to be seen as an end in itself and as a value mechanism that everything else serves. This would be ironic, as the leading agency in economic liberalisation is the TNC. But for all its many economic virtues and claims to far-sightedness and technological dynamism, it nevertheless remains the least transparent of all 'democratic' institutions and the one most openly committed to the practice of secrecy, that is, business secrecy. Its powers to hire and fire, invest or divest, locate or relocate, together with its forms of internal control, which are exceedingly commandist and authoritarian, make it far from democratic. The task clearly is to maximise the benefits from such institutions and simultaneously to minimise the social costs of their operation. To do so requires that they operate within a political and social framework not of their own making, but that of citizens and their preferred political institutions. It is from such a perspective that the response of the South to the global and national dilemmas we now face should be framed. If we do so we can help make globalisation serve the needs of all humanity, rather than the other way around; humanity serving globalisation in the interests of a few.

In conclusion, there are enormous opportunities for co-operation among countries of the South to promote social progress. The growing economic differentiation of the South adds to these opportunities, as they expand on its diversity and differing national capacities. As the South Centre has indicated after careful review:

There are enormous unexploited opportunities for co-operation among countries of the South to promote social progress. These opportunities are provided
by the great diversity in their history, culture, resource endowments, development experience and stages of economic advance . . . The countries of the South
have also much to learn from and teach each other. Their distinctive development experiences constitute a veritable treasure house of knowledge. In this
regard, knowledge of successful experiences to emulate may be as instructive
as that of the failed policies to shun. (South Centre, 1998, p. 143)

Notes

1. The empirical data show that despite the unprecedented growth in global pro-
    duction and consumption in recent decades, the unevenness and inequalities
    of this growth are very evident. As the UNDP has observed, whereas in 1960,
    20 per cent of the world's people who lived in the richest countries had 30
    times the income of the poorest 20 per cent, by 1995 it was 82 times as much!
    In Latin America and the Caribbean, the difference in average income be-
    tween the wealthiest quintile of the population and the poorest rose from 30
    times in the 1970s to 60 times today. As the UNDP goes on to observe, fre-
    quently these inequalities overlap: the poor and the rich, men and women, ru-
    ral and urban, and ethnic and political affiliation. These inequalities also oc-
    cur within the rich countries. The US Census Bureau reported in 1996 the
    widest gap between rich and poor since the end World War Two. While a few
    developing countries are now classed as emerging nations because of their
    spectacular growth, ten times as many developing countries are still ex-
    cluded. Estimates are that one-quarter of the world's population remains in
    severe human poverty while about one-third suffers from income poverty, i.e.
    survive on less US$1 per day (UNDP, 1998). While poverty has fallen more in
    the last half-century than in the previous five centuries, child death rates
    have halved over the past decade, malnutrition has declined by one-third,
    and the number of children out of primary school has fallen from over one-
    half to one-quarter, yet 160 million children are out of school, and half a mil-
    lion die in child birth (at rates ten to 100 times greater than in industrial
    countries). (UNDP, 1998)
    PAHO (1998) data also reveal that in the Americas, vaccination campaigns,
    improved nutrition, better and safer water and sanitation programmes and
    improved health facilities have led to significant improvements in the health
    of the people. However, the gap in health between the rich and poor coun-
    tries still exists. The infant mortality rate in Haiti is more than three times
    the regional average. Chronic diseases have assumed greater importance in
    the poorer countries. And, for the region as a whole, the number of AIDS
    cases represents half of the global total. Real prices of commodities traded in-

ternationally are now 45 per cent below the level in the 1980s, and 10 per cent below the lowest level of the Great Depression in 1932. Barriers to developing countries exports to the industrialised countries are estimated to cost them $60 billion annually. On average the Uruguay Round has reduced tariffs for industrial countries exports to 20–25 per cent, but for developing countries exports it remains at 45 per cent. Developing countries also face higher levels of tariffs on items processed from their raw materials (tariff escalation), discouraging the industrialisation of these commodities. There are as well considerable non-tariff barriers placed against their export, such as anti-dumping measures, and the special arrangements for trade in items of concern to them, like textiles and agricultural commodities. While global trade is growing faster than global income, for 44 developing countries it is declining. For the least developed countries, whose population is one-tenth of world population, their share has halved over the past 15 years and is now only 0.3 per cent.

2. As the Malaysian Prime Minister, Dr. Mahathir, has observed:
   'Despite dealing in billions and trillions of dollars, we do not know who they are, how they trade, where they trade and who invests in them. It is only when they fail, as in the Long-Term Capital Management case, that we learn about them and their massive trading.'
   (As cited in M. Khor, 'APEC Meeting Ends With Call For Hedge-Fund Review', *Third World Economics*, No. 198, December 1–15, 1998)

References

Benn, D., 1998, 'Globalization and the North-South Divide: Power Asymmetries in Contemporary International Economic Relations'; paper presented at the Conference on the Politics of Globalisation, Cornell University, N.Y., October.

Kennedy, P., 1998, 'On Thinking and Writing About the Future'; presentation at ACWS/ASIL Summer Workshop as cited in Lee, K. 'Globalisation and Health Policy', London School of Hygiene and Tropical Medicine, Discussion Paper No. 1, August.

Khor, M., 1998, 'APEC Meetings End With Call For Hedge-Fund Review', *Third World Economics*, No. 1998, December 1–15.

South Centre, 1998, 'Towards An Economic Platform for the South', Geneva.

Sutcliffe, R., 1998, 'Capitalism Sans Frontière? – A Critical Review of UNCTAD's World Investment Report 1998', *Third World Economics*, Issue No. 198, December 1–15.

Thomas, C.Y., 1998A, 'Globalisation, Structural Adjustment and Security: The Collapse of the Post-Colonial Development State in the Caribbean', *Global Development Studies*, Winter-Spring, pp. 67–84.

_____. 1998B, 'Towards a Progressive Economic Progamme in the Context of Globalisation'; paper presented at the PNP 60th Anniversary Symposium, Kingston, Jamaica, September.

_____. 1998C, 'The International Dimensions of Development'; paper presented to the University of Texas Medical Branch and WHO Collaborating Centre for International Health – PAHO/WHO Seminar on 'Health & Human Development in the New Global Economy: Experiences, Opportunities and Risks in the Americas', Galveston, Texas, October 26–28.

_____. 1998D 'The Economic Development of the OECS in the Newly Emerging International Order'; presentation at the OECS Third Annual Conference on Development, St Kitts, Nov/Dec,

_____. 1998E, 'Caribbean Agriculture in the Age of Globalisation and Liberalisation' (Forthcoming)

_____. 1998F 'Globalisation and Its Implications for Small States', chapter to be included in Howe, G., ed., *Globalisation, Development and Change in Caribbean Society* (Forthcoming)

3

Globalisation and the North-South Divide

Power Asymmetries in Contemporary International Economic Relations

D E N I S   B E N N

During the past decade, the phenomenon of globalisation has emerged as a dominant feature of contemporary international economic relations. At the same time, it has accentuated the polarisation between the developed and the developing countries as they seek to promote and defend competing economic interests. This paper will therefore analyse the nature of the globalisation process, the basis of the growing division between North and South, and identify approaches designed to create a truly interdependent international economic system geared to the satisfaction of the needs of both developed and developing countries.

Although the concept of globalisation has gained increased currency in the literature on contemporary international economic relations, as R.J. Barry Jones[1] has pointed out, it has given rise to a number of different interpretations which have often resulted in a blurring of the distinction between globalisation and related concepts such as interdependence. It is evident that the definition of globalisation has varied considerably depending on the perspective from which it is defined. For the purpose of this paper, however, globalisation is defined as the increased integration of trade, production and finance across national boundaries. In other words, it describes the process whereby economic transactions assume an increasingly transnational character and, therefore, cut across national boundaries and jurisdictions.

While it has gained increased prominence in recent years, globalisation is not an entirely new phenomenon since the international economic system experienced certain inchoate forms of economic integration during the era of colonialism, most notably during the nineteenth and early twentieth centuries, when vast areas of the developing world were incorporated into an imperial network of trade and production. In a sense, therefore, although the earlier phase was somewhat incomplete, due in part to the lower level of technological development prevailing at the time, the contemporary expression of globalisation may be said to have specific historical antecedents.

Nevertheless, the process of globalisation which has emerged in recent years has a number of distinctive characteristics and has assumed forms which were not entirely present in previous expressions of international economic integration. To be certain, globalisation is not a random phenomenon but is in fact a product of both technological progress and conscious economic policy.

In terms of the former, the profound technological revolution that has occurred in telecommunications, and particularly in information technology, created the conditions for increased cross-border communication and exchange and, therefore, laid the basis for an expansion of economic transactions among states on a global scale. The role of computer technology has been particularly important in facilitating instantaneous or real-time economic transactions which would have been inconceivable before the advent of the electronic age.

Quite apart from the role of technology in facilitating the process, globalisation has been promoted by conscious economic policy on the part of the developed countries. They have sought to universalise the application of neo-classical economic principles in terms of the promotion of private sector initiatives and unfettered liberalisation based on the primacy of market forces. In fact, the promotion of neo-classical economic orthodoxy, which underpins the process of globalisation, was first advanced at the national level and, subsequently, at the international level in two distinct, though related, phases.

Beginning in the 1980s, the introduction of economic stabilisation and structural adjustment programmes (SAPs) in the developing countries, under the sponsorship of the IMF and the World Bank, was specifically geared to reorienting these economies towards increased reliance on the private sector and increased market liberalisation, on the ground that such an orientation would result in greater economic efficiency thus laying the basis for a more sustained pattern of development. During the period between 1980 and 1994, a large number of developing countries had been forced to accept the logic of private sector-led development and market liberalisation and were, therefore, already predisposed to participate in a global economic system that was increasingly being shaped by these principles.

In addition to action at the national level aimed at reorienting the economies of the developing countries towards free market economics, through the instrumentality of economic stabilisation and SAPs, the developed countries consciously sought to construct the philosophical and institutional foundations for globalisation by initiating the Uruguay Round of multilateral trade negotiations which was launched during the GATT ministerial meeting held in Punta del Este in 1986.

This new round of multilateral trade negotiations, which was launched at the insistence of the developed countries in the face of sluggish economic growth and declining competitiveness of their economies during the 1980s, was designed to liberalise global trade and economic relations in order to expand investment opportunities and increase market access for goods and services produced by the developed countries. In fact, the developed countries sought to include a number of new elements in the negotiations which had not been addressed in previous rounds of negotiation. Overall, they focused their efforts on issues such as the rights of establishment as a basis for legitimising the operations of transnational corporations in the developing countries; the expansion of services, particularly in financial sector; and intellectual property rights in order to protect their technological superiority and also to ensure increased returns on the use of such technology by the developing countries. The developing countries, on the other hand, sought to oppose the introduction of these issues which they felt would lead to agreements which might be inimical to their economic interests.

Because of their significance for the process of globalisation, it is important to analyse the salient features of specific agreements concluded in the context of the Uruguay Round, which was finalised in 1994, and also the institutional arrangements that have been elaborated, in the form of the WTO, to manage a progessively liberalised global trading regime. Special attention will be paid to the agreements related TRIPS; the GATS; TRIMS; and the institutional arrangements in the WTO itself, although other issues such as agriculture, textiles, balance of payments support, safeguards, anti-dumping, subsidies, countervailing duties, and dispute settlement were also the subject of negotiation.

The TRIPS agreement seeks to provide increased multilaterally agreed protection for patents, copyrights, trade marks, industrial design, geographical indications, integrated circuits and undisclosed information (trade secrets) along the lines of the regulations existing in the developed countries, most notably the US. Consequently, although many developing countries have national legislation governing intellectual property which reflects their particular needs and circumstances, they will be required to enact legislation and adopt appropriate agreements in order to comply with the provisions of the TRIPS regime.

The TRIPS agreement, which was in fact assiduously promoted by the developed countries in response to pressures exerted by their corporate lobbies, is designed essentially to prevent the developing countries from gaining unauthorised access to the technology of the developed countries for fear that access to such technology could erode the competitiveness of the developed countries. Its effect, however, would be to protect what Samir Amin has called the 'technological monopoly' of the North vis-à-vis the South, and thus reinforce a division of labour in the global economy in which the North continues to enjoy a dominance in the production of high-tech goods and services with the South producing, by and large, agricultural commodities and low value-added products. Of course, the strengthening of the IPR system reflected in the TRIPS agreement is likely to lead to increased returns to the owners of technology in the North and, therefore, have a redistributive effect in the international economy.

Yet ironically, despite the insistence by the developed countries on monopoly rights and privileges in respect of technology owned by them, they continue to defend the acquisition of patent rights in respect of improvements effected by them on genetic material originating in the developing countries. This principle has far-reaching implications, given the fact that the developing countries account for the bulk of the world's biodiversity and have been a major provider of genetic material to the North. The irony of the situation is that the developing countries will be required to pay royalties to access improvements in genetic material originating in their countries. This has important consequences, given the potential of biotechnology, which is perhaps the next great scientific frontier, and which some analysts estimate will account for a sizeable proportion of the global economy in the future. In other words, the developed countries have secured monopoly protection for their own technology while seeking to deny the right of the developing countries to protect their genetic material. This situation would need to be monitored closely in order to prevent the appropriation by the North of critical resources available in the developing world.

It is also important to note that the negotiation of the TRIPS agreement was quite one-sided and lacking in transparency, with the developed countries determined to secure acceptance of their position in the face of objections from the developing countries. The negotiation formula which was adopted served to exclude the majority of developing countries from the negotiations which, in a sense, is symptomatic of recent trends in North-South discussions.

In the case of the GATS, the agreement provides a multilateral framework for liberalising trade in services and also laid down guidelines to govern subsequent negotiations in a number of important sectors. In the specific area of financial services, which have become a major dimension of globalisation, agreement was reached on a number of measures which impose stringent conditions for the liberalisation of the sector, including the granting of market access in respect of services such as insurance, data-processing, and ancillary services relating to banking and finance.

In contrast to these intrusive provisions, which will serve to open the developing countries to significant competition from transnational corporations involved in this sector, the developed countries refused to accept the free movement of labour in which the developing countries have a significant competitive advantage. In fact, the annex of GATS on the Movement of Natural Persons makes only minor concessions for those seeking employment in the developed countries by granting temporary access to highly skilled professionals engaged in the provision of services.

The steadfast refusal by the developed countries to accept the free movement of labour is clearly inconsistent with the logic of economic liberalisation, which should be premised on the free movement of all factors of production and, therefore, underlines the partial and selective manner in which liberalisation is applied in the context of globalisation.

It should be pointed out that, apart from immigration considerations, as will be shown later, the position of the developed countries is in part motivated by the fact that their current economic strategy is premised on continued access to cheap labour in the low-wage economies of the South. The removal of existing constraints on the free movement of labour would clearly negate such a strategy.

In any event, on the issue of financial services, the liberalisation of this sector, particularly in terms of the movement of short-term capital, can generate significant instability in the economies of the developing countries, as the Mexican peso crisis of 1994 and the East Asian financial crisis of 1997 have shown. In fact, it was US pressure during the negotiations that led to the inclusion in the Agreement of even more stringent provisions on financial liberalisation by holding out for increased concessions from the developing countries.

The agreement on TRIMS, which governs the treatment of foreign investment, represents a major victory for the developed countries since it provides increased legitimacy for foreign investment and, more particularly, the operations of transnational corporations. The negotiation of the agreement reflected a number of major differences between the developed countries, which sought to promote the interests of foreign investment, and the developing countries, which emphasised the transfer of technology in support of their development and the need to prevent foreign investors from adopting restrictive business practices.

It is worth noting that following the adoption of the agreement, the developed countries mounted a campaign to secure the adoption of a comprehensive multilateral agreement on investment (MAI) designed to grant national treatment to foreign investors. The developing countries have, however, maintained their strong opposition to the proposal since it is felt that such a provision would undermine the position of domestic enterprises by exposing them to unfair competition from transnational corporations from the North. The proposal which is currently being held in abeyance is therefore likely to continue to generate significant controversy between North and South if it is again proposed for negotiation.

The establishment of the WTO itself, largely at the insistence of the developed countries, represented an important institutional achievement of the Uruguay Round. Essentially it will serve as a forum for the negotiation of international trade agreements and also monitor the implementation of the various agreements in keeping with the objective of promoting an increasingly liberalised global trading regime. It should be mentioned that the creation of the WTO as an autonomous institution, outside the framework of the UN system, was done largely at the insistence of the developed countries. This decision reflects a continuing trend on the part of the developed countries to move decisions on global economic issues away from democratic forums such as the UN and to locate decision-making functions in institutions such as the WTO, the IMF, and the World Bank – which are under the control of the developed countries. Indeed, it is significant that under the terms of the agreement emanating from the Uruguay Round, the WTO is encouraged to co-operate with the IMF and the World Bank in order to achieve greater coherence in global economic policy. The developing countries are therefore wary that the provision could lead to the imposition of even more stringent conditionalities, further constraining their development options. In fact, the WTO, the IMF, and the World Bank constitute a triad of forces which defend and sustain the ideological underpinnings of the process of globalisation as it has evolved in recent years.

The new multilateral trading regime resulting from the Uruguay Round agreements, which will be subject to a process of ongoing negotiations in the WTO, has clearly moved away from the preferential arrangements conceded in the past agreements which explicitly recognised the need for concessions to the developing countries by virtue of their narrow specialisation, their underdeveloped productive capacity, and their overall low level of development. Instead, the new regime envisages a reciprocity-based system in which all countries, developed and developing, regardless of their level of development, would, by and large, compete on an equal basis. As such, it has resulted in a highly skewed international trading system with significant power asymmetries between the developed and the developing countries.

Since the WTO agreement provides for a process of ongoing negotiations, the developed countries have sought to bring a number of new issues to the negotiating table. Among the most important of these issues are trade and environment; trade and labour standards – the so-called 'social clause'; competition policy; and procurement. However, it is clear that there are fundamental differences between the positions of the developed and the developing countries on these issues.

In terms of the environmental issue, the developing countries are concerned that the developed countries will seek to impose environmental standards which will operate in a manner that is likely to further restrict their access to the markets of the developed countries. In the view of the developing countries, the imposition of stringent environmental standards at this stage of their development could result in an increase in their production costs thus eroding their comparative advantage.

Similarly, the developing countries are suspicious that the promotion of labour standards, which are ostensibly designed to abolish labour practices that violate fundamental human rights, including child labour, may be motivated less by humanitarian concerns than by a desire to impose further restrictions on the export capability of the developing countries and thus continue, in another guise, an essentially protectionist policy towards the developing countries.

More important still is the debate on competition policy. It is clear that the developed countries see the adoption of such a policy as a means of facilitating foreign investment and legitimising the activities of transnational corporations. On the other hand, the developing countries view competition policy as a means of gaining access to technology and imposing suitable controls over the restrictive business practices of transnational corporations. The situation is further complicated by recent research which indicates that the assumptions regarding competition policy in the developed countries do not apply in the same way in the case of the developing countries, in view of the existence of different structural conditions in these countries. The developed and the developing countries therefore remain in fundamental opposition on this issue.

Given the precedents created in the case of the TRIPs and TRIMs agreements, the developed countries are likely to continue to seek to use the WTO as a basis for the discussion of new issues, some of which have not traditionally fallen under the trade sector, and also to establish new agreements on these subjects within the WTO framework. Given this reality, it is important to examine the approaches adopted by the developed and the developing countries to the negotiations during the Uruguay Round as well as in the ongoing discussion of issues within the WTO framework since the conclusion of the Uruguay Round agreements.

It is evident that the developed countries have had from the very inception of the negotiations a clear conception of the elements of a multilateral trading system that reflects their economic interests and have formulated a systematic plan of action and a strategy for promoting this objective. In pursuing this strategy, the developed countries invariably sought to introduce into the negotiations, under the guise of conducting studies or carrying out preliminary exchanges, issues which, although initially opposed by the developing countries, eventually formed the basis of new multilateral regimes. This is true of the TRIPs, the GATS and the TRIMs, which had initially been opposed by the developing countries. In other cases, such as in the telecommunications agreement adopted during the first ministerial meeting of the WTO held in Singapore in December 1996, the developed countries have been able to force a decision on the issue by forging a prior consensus among themselves and by presenting the developing countries with a virtual *fait accompli*. In the actual negotiations the developed countries, particularly the United States, have also sought to apply bilateral pressure on the developing countries, including threat of the application of Section 301 of the US Trade Act which sanctions retaliation against countries for unfair trading practices directed at the US.

The developing countries, on the other hand, adopted a defensive stance during the negotiations by seeking to resist the initiatives advanced by the developed countries without having an overall vision and plan of action that could be advanced as a counter to the position of the developed countries. Based on the results of the Uruguay Round negotiations, this strategy has clearly failed. The developing countries would therefore need to adopt a more proactive stance in respect of ongoing and future negotiations being carried out within the WTO framework. In this regard, they would need to seek to modify elements of the agreements which prove to be detrimental to their interests and at the same time promote issues of special interest to them, including the free movement of labour, the regulation of restrictive business practices of foreign investors, and the protection of plant varieties which are susceptible to genetic engineering for which patents may be obtained under the terms of the Uruguay Round agreements.

In pursuing this strategy, the developing countries would need to utilise the resources and capacities available in institutions of the developing world such as South Centre and Third World Network (TWN), in their effort to formulate a comprehensive strategy to guide their approach to the implementation of the Uruguay Round agreements. They also need to strengthen their negotiating stance in ongoing and future negotiations within the WTO on issues such as trade and the environment; subsidies, safeguards, professional services, telecommunications, and government procurement; audio visual and marine services as well as other service sectors; agricultural reform; implementation of the textile agreement; patents; and the review of the TRIMs agreement. More important still, they would need to insist on the adoption of transparent and democratic procedures in respect of the negotiations in order to ensure the participation of all member countries, many of which are currently excluded under the infamous 'green room' process which is confined to a limited number of representatives.

Fortuitously, the position of the developing countries has been strengthened to some extent by the 'debacle in Seattle' resulting from the failure of the developed countries at the WTO Ministerial Meeting in Seattle in December 1999 to force agreement on a new round of negotiations in the face of the opposition of the developing countries, the US labour movement, and significant elements of the NGO community. However, the developing countries will need to continue to be vigilant in order to ensure that this advantage is not dissipated in future negotiations within the WTO in Geneva.

Having analysed the main elements of the Uruguay Round agreements and the possible strategies to be pursued by the developing countries to maximise the benefits to be derived from their participation in the new multilateral trading regime, it is important to highlight some of the most significant features of the process of globalisation currently under way.

Firstly, under the new dispensation, foreign direct investment (FDI) carried out mainly through transnational corporations has assumed increased importance. It is estimated, for example, that during the past 16-year period between 1981 and 1996, there was a six-fold increase in FDI flows in the world economy, amounting to $349 billion in 1996 compared with an annual average investment of $50 billion during the period 1981–1985. In the case of the developing countries, these flows also increased six-fold between 1981 and 1996, amounting to $129 billion or 31 per cent of global flows.[2]

In this context, it should also be noted that there has been an increased tendency on the part of corporations in the developed countries to shift physical production from the high-wage developed countries to the developing countries where the existence of an abundant supply of cheap labour allows corporations to increase their return on capital, both in terms of the benefits derived from production in low-wage economies and from the value added derived from the sale of products which are produced in the developing countries and sold in the developed countries. This process of 'delocation' of industry, as Michel Chossudovsky[3] has termed it, has contributed to corporate downsizing in the developed countries, which has been occurring with increasing frequency in recent years.

As William Greider (1997) has pointed out, transnational corporations have engaged in a kind of global arbitrage of labour whereby they are able to bid down its price by generating competition among the labour markets of various developing countries and are therefore able to exploit cheap labour on this basis.

Moreover, although the decision by transnationals to locate their production operations in different countries was initially motivated by a desire to exploit cheap labour, the strategy of spreading their operations among different countries has enabled the corporations to 'hedge their bets', since it gives them the flexibility to shift production from one country to another in the event that political, economic or social difficulties threaten to disrupt their operations in a particular country.

The expansion of corporate activities on a global scale is also characterised by increasing mergers among various entities and by the development of multi-faceted ownership structures in which individual corporations own or manage a number of entities. For example, apart from the fact that it is a major telecommunications corporation, VIACOM is the parent company of Paramount Studios, a range of motion picture theatres and also Blockbuster Videos, even though these entities function under their independent names.

It should also be noted that the current pattern of global corporate investment has generated growing tension between capital and labour, since the former has an interest in accessing cheap labour in order to maximise profits, whereas the latter has a vested interest in preserving jobs which are lost as a result of investment abroad.

The shift of physical production structures to the developing countries has allowed the developed countries to move to a new forms of specialisation in the more profitable high-tech sectors involving various service functions, most notably computer technology and financial services. This new division of labour has also enabled the developed countries to reap a dual benefit: 1) on the one hand, they continue to enjoy the profits from the enterprises located on the developing countries which, as mentioned earlier, have succeeded in maximising their returns based on the exploitation of cheap labour, while 2) at the same time they benefit from the virtual monopoly enjoyed by the developed countries in a number of high-tech areas as well as financial services. In the case of the latter, this has produced super profits deriving from a number of speculative interventions in the developing countries, as the 1994 Mexican peso crisis and the 1997 East Asian financial crisis have demonstrated.[4]

Bolstered by the logic of free-market economics, which is embodied in the Uruguay Round agreements and supported by the economic philosophy of the IMF, the World Bank as well as other institutions in the developed countries, globalisation is generating new patterns of production, trade and finance, and a division of labour in the international economic system that will further reinforce the economic power of the North *vis-à-vis* the South and thus perpetuate a pattern of dependence that will operate as a major constraint on the development possibilities of the developing countries.

It should be noted, however, that while globalisation was also supposed to benefit the developing countries, particularly those with a fairly developed productive capacity, it has in fact generated significant financial instability in the international economy as the East Asian crisis has illustrated. For this reason, it is important to examine the nature of that crisis and to seek to derive from the experience, lessons which might lead us to revisit the assumptions of globalisation or, at least, to introduce modifications in the operation and management of the global economy that will avoid further financial crises.

Prior to the emergence of the Asian financial crisis, which may be said to have begun with the devaluation of the Thai baht in July 1997, the so-called newly industrialising countries of the region had achieved spectacular levels of growth, averaging almost seven per cent a year during the period 1991 to 1996. Although there was an ongoing debate on the relative importance of the role of government intervention and the adoption of industrial policies in stimulating investment, there was little doubt that these countries represented exemplary models of modern economic success. Moreover, the World Bank study on the East Asian Miracle,[5] published in 1993, concluded that the countries had pursued sound macroeconomic policies, even if in some cases they had engaged in a degree of 'financial repression' in order to stimulate the growth of certain economic sectors which were considered critical for achieving an accelerated pace of development.

Despite the attempt by the developed countries and international institutions such as the IMF and the World Bank to attribute the crisis entirely to factors such as crony capitalism, weak corporate management, poor banking practices, over-investment in construction and large current account deficits, it is clear that while some of these factors were relevant, speculative attacks on the currencies of the region and the inflow and outflow of short-term capital which occurred in the context of a process of rapid financial liberalisation also constituted critical contributory factors in triggering the crisis.

The subsequent IMF prescriptions which followed the logic of unfettered market liberalisation clearly compounded the crisis. Apart from its effort to restore financial stability through an increase in interest rates; the imposition of a restrictive monetary policy; the closure of highly indebted banks and other financial institutions; cuts in government expenditure; and the extraction of a commitment from the governments to assume responsibility for private sector debts owed to foreign creditors, the thrust of the IMF policy was also aimed at prying open the economies of the region. It is interesting to note, for example, that the countries of the region, most notably Korea and Indonesia, have been forced to concede increased foreign ownership of a number of key sectors of the economy, which represents a long-standing objective of the developed countries that they had failed to achieve in previous bilateral negotiations with these countries and in the context of the WTO negotiations.

It is also not surprising that both the IMF and the US strongly opposed the proposed $100 billion East Asian Fund, which the countries in crisis together with Japan had agreed to launch at the outset of the crisis in an effort to restore financial stability in the region on the basis of regionally agreed criteria and conditions, since they felt that such an initiative would weaken the role of the Fund in imposing conditionalities which were not only influenced by a neo-classical economic philosophy, but were also supportive of the interests of the developed countries. For these reasons, the policies of the IMF in seeking to address the crisis in the region have come under increased attack and have been blamed for converting a financial crisis into a full blown economic recession.

While the IMF continues to advocate further financial liberalisation, a number of highly respected economists such as Paul Krugman of the Massachusetts Institute of Technology (MIT) have endorsed, at least as a temporary strategy, the imposition of exchange controls as a pragmatic measure for dealing with the crisis. Indeed, in an effort to protect the value of the currency and to prevent further capital outflows, Malaysia embarked on wide-ranging policy reforms, including the introduction of foreign exchange controls which have brought a measure of stability to the economy. It is significant that, despite the doubts initially expressed by economic purists wedded to the tradition of neo-classical economics, analysts have now conceded that the policy was indeed a success.

In the aftermath of the crisis there is a clear recognition that financial liberalisation would require the introduction of strengthened institutional arrangements to ensure effective management of the process. In addition, there is also a growing consensus in both developed and developing countries in support of the adoption of measures to control the inflow and outflow of short-term capital, which can induce significant instability. Indeed, countries such as Mexico, following the experience of the 1994 peso crisis, have introduced special measures for dealing with short-term capital flows in recognition of their destabilising effect on the economy. Even Chile had adopted such measures, even though it has recently eased some of the restrictions in this regard.

It is also significant that, as the effects of the East Asian crisis spread to other countries such as Russia, South Africa, Brazil, and even parts of the developed world on the basis of a domino effect, questions have been raised about the viability and efficacy of the unfettered application of market liberalisation, which has informed the process of globalisation.

There is also increasing recognition of the need to create a new global financial structure to deal, among other things, with the massive cross-border movement of capital – estimated to be in the region of US$1.3 trillion a day – which is currently regulated largely by the operation of market forces, and also to avoid major economic crises or, at least, to ensure the orderly management of such crises when they occur. Separate proposals on this issue have been advanced, on the one hand, by the UN Committee for Development Planning (CDP) and on the other, by the US Treasury and the Federal Reserve Chairman, Alan Greenspan, although the two sets of proposals are inspired by different conceptions of the needs of the situation since the latter seems to envisage a more intrusive IMF. The developing countries should insist that any reform of the existing international financial system should ensure their increased participation in the decision-making process.

The East Asian crisis, which has wrought severe economic damage and has affected the lives of millions of people in the most populous region of the world, has provided a number of important insights into the strengths and weaknesses of current approaches to globalisation. At a philosophical level, it would seem that globalisation, which is based on an ethic of neo-liberalism, is constructed on a flawed intellectual foundation. Unlike the situation in a national polity where there is recognition of a societal responsibility for ensuring some degree of equity and protecting the common good, invariably through the action of government, with globalisation there is no corresponding supranational authority vested with the responsibility for ensuring equity among states participating in the international economic system. Consequently, what prevails at the international level is a system of open competition among unequals, which inevitably favours the strong over the weak. Indeed, in the context of the assertion of an uncompromising neo-liberalism, the developed countries have sought to limit the power and influence of international institutions such as the UN, which are at least disposed to the principle of equity, for fear that they might stand in the way of the march of globalisation. In other words, the extension of the principles applicable in a national polity to the international arena has been partial and incomplete since it does not include mechanisms which exist at the national level to guarantee social equity in the context of the operation of a highly competitive economic system.

Ironically, the negative effects of a global economic system created to facilitate the continued economic dominance of the developed countries could well produce global economic instability that would adversely affect the economic interests of all countries – including the developed countries – unless the international community takes urgent steps to remove the glaring power asymmetries inherent in a flawed process of globalisation that has dominated international economic relations in recent years.

It should be emphasised that the problem does not necessarily lie with globalisation itself but with the form that globalisation has taken, leading to growing income disparities between the developed and the developing countries and being quite indifferent to these disparities and the extreme forms of economic and social deprivation which it has produced. It is also quite clear that the market cannot by itself guarantee economic stability and that some form of multilateral intervention by governments will be necessary to ensure economic rationality in the operation of the international economic system.

At this critical historical juncture, there is an urgent need to articulate a development vision that will seek to promote a more sustained pattern of development in the South and also a more humane and equitable global economic order. Both the North and the South have an abiding interest in pursuing this objective since it is vital to the promotion of economic prosperity and the preservation of international peace and security.

Notes

1. Jones, R.J. Barry, *Globalization and Interdependence in the Global Economy: Rhetoric and Reality* (Pinter Publishers, 1995)
2. South Centre, 'Foreign Direct Investment, Development and the New Global Economic Order: A Policy Brief for the South' (1997, pp. 17–18)
3. For further discussion on this subject, see Michel Chossudovsky, *The Globalisation of Poverty: Impacts of the IMF and World Bank Reforms* (Malaysia: Third World Network, 1997, pp. 75-98); and also William Greider, *One World, Ready or Not – the Manic Logic of Global Capitalism* (Penguin Books, 1997, pp. 51, 57 and 8–89)
4. A considerable body of literature has already been produced on the financial crisis in East Asia. However, useful insights on the nature of the crisis are provided in the UNCTAD Trade and Development Report 1998; Gill, Ranjit *Asia Under Siege: How the Asian Miracle Went Wrong* (Singapore: Epic Management Services Pte Ltd, 1998); Mahatir, Mohamad, *The Challenge of Turmoil* (Pelanduk Publications, 1998); and the various articles on the subject in *Third World Resurgence*, (Issue No.96 Third World Network).
5. See the World Bank, *The East Asian Miracle, Economic Growth and Public Policy*, (Oxford University Press, 1993, pp. 105–147)

References

Amin, Samir, *Capitalism in the Age of Globalisation: The Management of Contemporary Society* (London and New York: Zed Books, 1997)

Bhagwati, Jagdish, *A Stream of Windows: Unsettling Reflections on Trade, Immigration and Democracy* (MIT press, 1998)

Chossudovsky, Michel, *The Globalisation of Poverty: Impacts of the IMF and World Bank Reforms* (Malaysia: Third World Network, 1997)

Dunning, John H. and Khalil A. Hamdani, eds., *The New Globalism and Developing Countries* (United Nations University Press, 1997)

Gil-Diaz, Francisco, 'The Origins of Mexico's 1994 Financial Crisis', *The Cato Journal*, Volume 17, No. 3

Gill, Ranjit, *Asia Under Seige: How the Asia Miracle went Wrong* (Singapore: Epic Management Services Pte Ltd., 1998)

Greenspan, Alan, 'The Globalisation of Finance', *The Cato Journal*, Volume 17, No. 3

Greider, William, *One World, Ready or Not – the Manic Logic of Global Capitalism* (Penguin Books, 1997)

Hanke, Steve H., 'How to Establish Monetary Stability in Asia', *The Cato Journal*, Volume 17, No. 3

Henderson, Callum, *Asia Falling? Making Sense of the Asian Currency Crisis and Its Aftermath* (McGraw-Hill, 1998)

Hoekman, Bernard and Michel Kosteki, *The Political Economy of the World Trading System: From GATT to WTO* (Oxford University Press, 1995)

Khor, Martin, 'Countering the North's New Foreign Investment Treaty', *Third World Resurgence*, No. 64

Korten, David, *When Corporations Rule the World* (Kumarian Press, Inc. and Benett Koehler Publishers Inc., 1995)

Krugman, Paul, 'Part 2: Hong Kong's Hard Lesson', in *Fortune*, September 28, 1998

Jones, R.J. Barry, *Globalisation and Interdependence in the International Political Economy: Rhetoric and Reality* (Pinter Publishers, 1995)

Mahatir, Mohamad, *The Challenge of Turmoil* (Pelanduk Publications, 1998)

Meigs, A. James, 'Lessons for Asia from Mexico', *The Cato Journal*, Volume 17, No. 3

Mihevic, John, *The Market Tells Them So: The World Bank and Economic Fundamentalism in Africa* (Malaysia: Third World Network, 1995)

Milner, Helen V., 'International Political Economy: Beyond Hegemonic Stability', *Foreign Policy* (Special Edition), No. 110, Spring 1998

Ostry, Sylvia, *The Post Cold War Trading System: Who's on First, A Twentieth Century Fund Book* (University of Chicago, 1997)

Pennar, Karen, 'Two Steps Forward, One Step Back', *Business Week*, August 24–31, 1998

Rodrik, Dani, *Has Globalisation Gone too Far*, Institute of International Economics, 1997

Sacks, Jeffrey, 'International Economics: Unlocking the Mysteries of Globalisation', *Foreign Policy* (Special Edition), Spring 1998

South Centre, *Liberalisation and Globalisation: Drawing Conclusions for Development*, 1996

South Centre, *Foreign Direct Investment, Development and the New Global Economic Order – A Brief for the South*, 1997

South Centre, *The TRIPs Agreement – A Guide for the South*, November 1997

South Centre, *Towards an Economic Platform for the South*, September, 1998

Stiglitz, Joseph and Lyn Squire, 'International Development – Is It Possible?', *Foreign Policy* (Special Edition), No. 110, Spring 1998

UNCTAD, Trade and Development Board Report, 1998

Walt, Stephen M., 'International Relations: One World, Many Theories', *Foreign Policy* (Special Edition), No. 110, Spring 1998

World Bank, *The East Asian Miracle – Economic Growth and Public Policy* (Oxford University Press, 1993)

Yeager, Leland B., 'How to Avoid International Financial Crises', *The Cato Journal*, Volume 17, No. 3

4

The South in an Era
of Globalisation

JOHN OHIORHENUAN

Globalisation has many faces – in trade, finance, investment and production systems. It affects development thinking and action, relegating ethical, equity, and social concerns behind market considerations and reducing the autonomy of the state. Countries of the South need to come to terms with these phenomena by adjusting their development strategies.

Globalisation is, perhaps, the most widely discussed phenomenon today. It manifests itself dramatically in its effects on the lives of ordinary people. But globalisation is not just a destructive leviathan; it is also a powerful force for the improved material well-being of humankind. Dealing with the imperatives of globalisation, capitalising on its positives and mitigating its negatives, is perhaps the most important challenge for the new millennium.

Although its effects are felt worldwide in various degrees, the notion of globalisation is still not universally understood, and positions for or against are often taken on the basis of ideological leanings or gut feelings. For proponents, globalisation means the availability of cheap and rapid communications; cost effective transportation systems; and open markets that make possible the global dissemination of ideas, technology, and investment. It is argued further that as markets are integrated, investments flow more easily, competition is enhanced, prices are lowered, and living standards everywhere are improved. Opponents present globalisation as a foreign invasion that will destroy local cultures, regional co-operation and national traditions. As a first step, therefore, this article describes the main dimensions of globalisation, providing a factual basis for analysing its scope, effects, and implications for the South. Countries of the South, in particular, need to come to terms fully with globalisation in order to make the appropriate changes in their development agendas and strategies. This article also examines some of the implications of globalisation for developing countries and raises some questions about its ramifications for the policy-making autonomy of the state.

The Elements of Globalisation

Globalisation is first and foremost apprehended in economic and financial terms. In this sense, it may be defined as the broadening and deepening linkages of national economies into a worldwide market for goods, services and, especially, capital. As a result of changes in economic policy across a wide range of countries and a revolution in telecommunications and information technologies, the last fifteen years have witnessed dramatic increases in trade linkages and cross-border capital flows, as well as radical changes in form, structure, and location of production.

Furthermore, due to developments in media technology and communication, globalisation brings with it a growing tendency towards the universal homogenisation of ideas, cultures, values, and even lifestyles. One salient feature of cultural globalisation is seen in the ubiquitous spread of English. Although it is a mother tongue for only 380 million people, English is the language predominantly used in the world's books, academic papers, newspapers and magazines. It is transmitted all around the world by American radio, television, and films. More than 80 per cent of the postings on the Internet is now in English. As the language takes first place on the global landscape, more and more companies worldwide are making English competence a prerequisite for promotion and appointments.

In addition, running parallel with and even overarching the economic dynamics, there has been a growth of new supra-national policy regimes such as WTO, the Global Environmental Facility (GEF), and various global environmental conventions. There has also been a subtle realignment of older ones such as the Bretton Woods Institutions, the OECD, and even the United Nations. As globalisation takes hold, there is a felt need to regulate the process on the basis of a multilateral system of rules that are fair to all.

Trade

Over the last forty years, world trade in goods and services has consistently grown more rapidly than world output. As a result, close to 20 per cent of the total volume of world output is exported. These exports are worth $7 trillion, or about 23 per cent of the value of world output. Developing countries account for just over 30 per cent of global exports. Manufactures now account for over 60 per cent of developing country exports, compared to 40 per cent only ten years ago.

However, the secular buoyancy of trade is not enjoyed equally by all regions. Until the summer of 1997, Asia and Latin America had annual export growth rates of around 7 per cent and 5 per cent respectively over the last 25 years. But Africa has suffered an average annual decline of 1 per cent, and its share of world merchandise trade has fallen to about 2 per cent from around 6 per cent in the early 1980s. Latin America has maintained a share of about 5 per cent over this period while Asia's share had increased significantly from about 16 per cent to 27 per cent. Does the creation of the WTO raise prospects for the South to have a fair share in world trade? Trade liberalisation and the deregulation following the conclusion of the Uruguay Round and the establishment of the WTO were seen initially by developing countries as bringing in a new period of international prosperity in which they would share through improved access to markets. It can also be asserted that the WTO has indeed contributed to a more open, rule-based and predictable trading system, engendering negotiations to increase market access, settle disputes, and facilitate access to technology, information, and various services. But by and large developing countries continue to face significant obstacles to market access, including stiff tariffs. They are also subject to standards too high for them to meet due to their relatively lower levels of technological advancement.

Finance

Perhaps the most prominent face of globalisation is the rapid integration of financial markets over the last decade. Innovations in communications and computer-mediated technologies have made possible a vast array of new financial instruments and risk-management technologies. In addition, fixed exchange rates were abandoned in the early 1970s and financial markets were subsequently deregulated. The result has been a spectacular increase in cross-border capital flows. Cross-border transactions in bonds and equities were generally less than 10 per cent of GDP in 1980 for the major advanced economies; by 1996 they were generally over 100 per cent. The average daily turnover in foreign exchange markets, adjusted for local and cross-border double-counting, has risen sharply from about $15 billion in 1973 to about $200 billion in 1986 to over $1.3 trillion in 1995.

The last 25 years have seen a sharp rise in the growth of portfolio equity flows, particularly to the so-called emerging markets. From nothing in 1970, portfolio equity flows to developing countries were estimated at $46 billion in 1996 and $33 billion in 1997, the downturn being mainly the result of the East Asian financial crisis. Regional variations are also quite sharp, with Latin America and East Asia receiving 62 per cent of total portfolio equity flows to the developing countries.

Even more significant for developing countries is the changing character of net long-term resource flows. First, private capital is now dominant, contributing 85 per cent in 1996 versus 45 pert cent in 1990. Second, portfolio flows constitute almost 30 per cent of total non-debt private capital flows, a manifestation of the growing importance of non-bank financial institutions (insurance companies, mutual and pension funds, etc.) as sources of development finance.

Financial flows have vividly revealed some of the threats posed by globalisation. Uncontrolled financial movements, aided by high-tech communication instruments, have proved to be a volatile force that wrenches governments and populations alike. A crisis that began in Southeast Asia in July 1997 triggered panic among private capital controllers that by November had erased some $400 billion of value from the region's capital markets. In all the economies of the region, exports were affected, stock market capitalisation reduced, rates of foreign investment slowed, and currency values eroded. According to recent estimates (October 1998), since the crisis began, $1 trillion in loans had gone bad, $2 trillion in equity capitalisation for Asian stock markets had been vaporised, and $3 trillion in GDP growth had been lost. Social consequences are even more significant. In Indonesia alone, the crisis is likely to throw some 50 million people back into poverty.

Production

The global stock of FDI was $3.2 trillion in 1996, having grown at an annual average rate of 24 per cent from 1986–90 and 17 per cent from 1991–96. FDI inflows averaged about $28 billion in the 1970s, $50 billion in the first half of the 1980s, $142 billion in the second half, and $243 billion between

BOX 4.1
**Some Facts about Transnational Corporations and the
Global Economy (1995)**

- There are 39,000 TNCs, including 4,148 from developing countries. They have 270,000 affiliates, of which 119,765 are in developing countries.
- FDI stock at the end of 1995 was $2.7 trillion. Of this amount, 65 per cent was accounted for by France, Germany, Japan, the United Kingdom and the United States. Developing countries accounted for about 7.8 per cent of the world-wide FDI stock.
- The sales of foreign affiliates of TNCs in 1993 were estimated to be $6 trillion, compared with $4.7 trillion of world exports.
- China was the leading developing country recipient of FDI flows in 1995. South and South East Asia received 65 per cent of the total flows to developing countries, and Latin America and the Caribbean 27 per cent of the total flows.
- The largest 100 TNCs (excluding those in banking and finance) are estimated to account for about one-third of global FDI.
- World-wide cross-border mergers and acquisitions of all kinds doubled in value between 1988 and 1995, and accounted for 72 per cent of FDI outflows (42 per cent in the case of majority-held mergers and acquisition transactions).
- 75 to 80 per cent of all FDI stock in 1992 was in sectors requiring above average levels of human skill, capital or technology intensity.
- 50 to 55 per cent of all FDI in 1992 was in the tertiary (service) sector.
- FDI and strategic alliances are growing faster than other forms of international transactions.
- Some 73 per cent of the stock of inward investment at the end of 1995 was in developed countries, though developing countries accounted for 32 per cent of all new FDI. Central and Eastern Europe accounted for almost 4 per cent of world-wide inflows of FDI in 1995.
- Over the period 1991–1994, FDI from privatisation schemes in Central and Eastern Europe amounted to over $8.5 billion, or 49 per cent of the region's total FDI inflows. In the case of developing countries, privatisations amounted to $17.6 billion, or 6 per cent of their total FDI inflows in 1989–94.

Source: Dunning, 1997

1991 and 1996. Here again, there are marked disparities by region. Africa's share of FDI inflows was only 1.4 per cent of global inflows in 1996, compared to 11 per cent for Latin America and the Caribbean, and 13 per cent for South-East Asia. Indeed, the bulk of FDI flows occurs among the high-income countries – about 63 per cent, and ten countries account for 78 per cent of the total developing country share.

The growth of FDI underscores the enormous role of TNCs in economic activity worldwide. The value of goods and services produced by foreign affiliates was estimated at $7 trillion in 1995. Not surprisingly, production by TNCs is becoming the dominant mode of servicing foreign markets. With the dramatic fall in transport and communication costs over the last 40 years, firms are finding it efficient to locate different stages of production in different parts of the world. Foreign trade is becoming more and more intra-industry and intra-firm, especially for the advanced economies. The TNC has also become the quintessential vehicle for knowledge and technology transfer. Significantly, the global assets of TNCs were estimated at over $8 trillion in 1994, compared to global gross domestic investment of $5,681 billion. The main features of TNC activity are presented in box 4.1.

Intra-firm trade is increasingly becoming the leading edge of foreign trade. For the US, for instance, intra-firm trade accounted for over 35 per cent of exports and 40 per cent of imports in 1995. The US Federal Trade Commission estimates that, between 1983 and 1992, intra-firm trade accounted for 43 per cent of US-Europe trade and 71 per cent of US-Japan trade. With the evolution of the TNCs into a global network of interlocking activities, the nature of comparative advantage is changing from its old locational basis (country) to a new organisational basis (the firm). This development carries significant implications for the relationship between policy and market outcome.

Globalisation: Some Critical Considerations for the South

The implications of globalisation are not yet fully understood, even for the high-income economies. For countries of the South, the issues are considerably more complex because globalisation is radically changing the parameters of the development agenda. Three questions seem to be fundamental for the South. First, is globalisation rendering the notion of development redundant? Second, how does globalisation affect the relative autonomy of the developing country state in national policy-making? Third, will globalisation be regulated by a multilateral system of rules favourable to all?

Globalisation and the Idea of Development

From the earlier idea of development as growth, the prevailing paradigm insists on several qualifiers to drive home the notion that development is about people in social interaction and in interaction with other occupants of the planet, hence the increased use of terms such as 'sustainable development'; 'sustainable human development'; 'environmentally sustainable development'; 'equitable development', and so on. With or without qualifiers, however, the idea of development is supported by the teleological philosophy that means are pre-figured by ends; that development implies purposive action to get from an existing state to a desired state.

While globalisation is not completely new, the current era is located firmly in the context of a new market fetishism. Against the background of disenchantment with the results of 30 years of social engineering in developing countries, a 'neo-classical counter-revolution' was launched in the late 1970s to reassert the virtues of the market and the importance of 'getting prices right'. With the collapse of communism, the triumph of market over state was complete. The resultant tendency towards ideological homogeneity considerably reduces the intellectual space for the consideration of ethical and equity issues in social interaction and international relations.

Implicitly, the new market fetishism is elevating the notion of self-interest as the basis of market rationality to a 'take-no-prisoners' attitude in inter-personal and inter-country relations. The contemporary manifestation of market liberalism, in its pursuit of pure commercialism, appears to leave little room for charity or the generosity of spirit that used to be taken for granted as the essence of civilised behaviour. With no constraints beyond the ethics of respect for property rights, the post-Cold War market ideology justifies predatory behaviour as the natural tendency of humankind.

Despite the genuine concern of the international development community with the existential conditions of people in developing countries, the Darwinian logic of the market is also increasingly reflected in the discourse on development co-operation. In debates at the United Nations, powerful countries argue that the end of the Cold War has made the North-South distinction irrelevant, as such distinctions were merely a reflection of the Cold War ideological divide. The New World Order, they argue, is one of 'partnership' and each country is wholly responsible for its own destiny. Moreover, this new partnership is essentially a quid pro quo relationship except, perhaps, in purely humanitarian causes.

The declining level of Official Development Assistance (ODA) over the last decade is, at least partly, a result of the growing perception that development assistance is anachronistic. Aid budgets already short of the level agreed by the UN General Assembly, have shrunk further in recent years. As a group, the industrialised countries contribute 0.22 per cent of their GNP as opposed to the agreed level set at 0.7 per cent. This comes at a time when many developing countries have taken drastic measures to restructure their economies, even as the increase in foreign direct invest-ment falls short of compensating for the decline in development assistance. In 1997, all of sub-Saharan Africa received $3 billion and South Asia $4 billion. Aid channelled through the United Nations remains at a modest level of $5.5 billion a year.

It may also be argued that the increasing powers of those multilateral institutions with a 'one-dollar, one-vote' decision-making mechanism and the corresponding weakening of those with a 'one-country, one- vote' mechanism is symptomatic of an unabashed acceptance of plutocracy as a morally acceptable basis of global governance.

In the context of the high-income countries, Dani Rodrik makes an eloquent case for the re-affirmation of the 'social insurance' role of govern-ments. In his words:

'Globalisation... is part of a broader trend that we may call marketisation. The broader challenge for the 21st century is to engineer a new balance between market and society, one that will continue to unleash the creative energies of private entrepreneurship without eroding the social basis of co-operation.'

Development co-operation is in many ways the international relations analogue of social insurance. Just as social insurance has historically facilitated trade integration and multilateral liberalisation, so too has de-velopment co-operation helped to foster world peace, precarious as it may be. The phenomenon of declining ODA and the growing impatience with the endemic problems of developing countries is, perhaps, a logical outcome of globalisation. But it would be myopic to forget that globalisation by its nature tends to generate international market failures and social dislocation because it is uneven in intensity and scope and because it impacts differently on different classes of people.

Globalisation and the Relative Autonomy
of the Developing State

In Adam Smith's famous formulation, the pursuit of individual self-interest produces the best good for society. Advocates of the new market liberalism often go back to Smith as the oracle. It is often forgotten however, that Smith was emphatic in portraying 'large combinations of capital' as contradicting the realisation of market efficiency. More significantly, perhaps, is the fact that there is often a failure to acknowledge that Smith distrusted the state because he saw it as an institutional manifestation of the conspiracy of the rich and/or propertied against the poor and/or property-less. He did expect the state to provide an enabling institutional and infrastructural framework, and it is this dimension of his work that is said to justify the notion of a minimalist state.

However, the evolution of the state in the high-income countries has seen the full acceptance of its role in providing the social overhead capital that is necessary for the market to function reasonably effectively. Accordingly, while there may have been debate as to the neutrality or autonomy of the state (i.e. the extent to which it is a register of the balance of social forces), there was no serious questioning of its role in mediating internal social conflict whether negatively (as in repression) or positively (as in the provision of social services and safety nets). It was also broadly accepted that the state has pre-eminence in mediating between the domestic and external domains.

Globalisation fundamentally challenges the mediative role of the state *vis-à-vis* external forces. The combined effect of the global fluidity of finance capital, the growth of FDI, and the emergence of the global corporation is to undermine the economic sovereignty of states. Vincent Cable describes how highly mobile capital leads national regulators to cede control to global markets that are wholly unregulated (currency markets), lightly self-regulated (bond markets), or imperfectly regulated (multinational banking). (Cable, 1995) For instance, the management of exchange rates now depends less directly on government action than on the action of foreign exchange and securities traders. The recent experience of some East Asian economies and of Mexico in 1994 shows what can happen when international finance decides to pull out from a country for whatever reason.

While international trade as an element of globalisation is, perhaps, less spectacular than finance, it is in this area that the new constraints on the state are most visibly demonstrated. Globalisation is market-driven but, in the area of trade, it is clear that the process is significantly facilitated by the actions of states. The establishment of the rule-based multilateral trade regime embodied in the WTO is the result of a process in which the leading actors are government officials. The whole process engenders a tension, identified by Cable and Rodrick among others, between countries over domestic norms and social institutions. The main point for the developing country, however, is that the ability to take advantage of, or create opportunities and mitigate threats, is a function of the capacity and discretionary power of the state.

By broadening the notion of trade into trade-related issues, the Uruguay Round moved critical issues of economic policy such as foreign investment, intellectual property, technology, technical, health and safety standards, and a broad range of services onto the platform of international trade relations. It is of particular concern to developing countries that the negotiations tend to be heavily influenced by the powerful countries.

The rule-based trade regime imposes an additional burden on the countries of the South to build national capacity to project and protect national interests and to be more effective negotiators; to develop the capacity to comply with agreed obligations and exercise their rights; and to put in place a whole panoply of new institutional arrangements in order to be more competitive.

The declining autonomy of the state is not unique to developing countries. For instance, in the high-income countries, governments are under pressure to help their citizens adjust to the changes brought about by globalisation, even as the tax base to support public consumption is eroded by the imperatives of competitiveness. The difficulty of taxing increasingly footloose capital combined with the need to maintain comparatively low taxation levels tends to shrink the fiscal base. It is possible, as Cable observes, to resort to higher levels of deficit financing. But this strategy 'is eventually circumscribed by international financial markets: which foreign investors are willing to lend, and on what terms'.

For the developing country, the problem is compounded by the fact that the notion of an activist state, which is required to establish safety nets and lead the development process, is seen as *passé* intellectually and unfeasible practically. Intellectually, the activist state is incompatible with the ideology of liberalisation. Historically, the activist state has relied heavily on domestic and external resources for which it did not always pay full market value. It also requires an international policy context which allows considerable variation in development strategies and domestic policy regimes among countries.

The Managing Director of the IMF, in describing the organisation's prescription for the 'second generation' of reform, highlights implicitly the enormity of the challenge for developing countries. The four core elements of this policy regime – better fiscal adjustment, 'bolder' structural reforms, better government and strengthened financial institutions – all require a highly competent state machinery. Better fiscal adjustment includes reducing budget deficits and changing the composition of government expenditure to improve education and training, reform pension schemes and healthcare delivery and provide social safety nets. 'Bolder' structural reforms mean securing a smaller, better paid and more efficient civil service, undertaking extensive labour market as well as trade and regulatory reforms, and creating/reinforcing property rights regimes. Better government means improving transparency and accountability as well as ensuring reliable public services. Strengthening domestic financial institutions implies establishing appropriate prudential and oversight mechanisms.

Even this minimalist agenda shows quite clearly that, in Dunning's words, markets are not a free good; they cost resources to set up, to operate and to maintain. It has been aptly argued that a global economy requires stronger states. Globalisation promises more wealth in exchange for the readiness and willingness to change, adjust, be alert and have the capacity to move people, money and resources in and out of various arenas of economic activity. This calls for higher and not lower public investment in training and retraining. In conditions where the private sector is at a low level of development, the state must take the lead in building an adequate skills-base by training a critical mass of engineers, managers, lawyers, doctors, accountants and other professionals. The rapid speed at which economies are changing raises the need for effective safety nets to cater for those who fall through the cracks during the transition. By enhancing the mobility of money, goods, and services, globalisation increases the demand for public-sponsored goods and services such as social insurance, education, urban infrastructure, sanitation, police, public transportation, and telecommunications. The major challenge for the developing country is to find the resources to ensure a reasonably competent state and the resources to set up and maintain reasonably effective markets at the same time that the traditional providers of these resources are threatened by the forces of globalisation.

South-South Co-operation

Since the 1970s, developing countries have recognised the need for South-South partnerships consisting of Technical Co-operation among Developing

Countries (TCDC) and Economic Co-operation among Developing Countries (ECDC). The two interrelated approaches to development are intended to enable countries of the South to draw on the human and material resources within their borders in an effort to accelerate social and economic progress in the South.

For the past twenty years, South-South initiatives emphasised the formation of regional groupings across the South. Regional integration has enabled many countries to expand their market size and to accelerate the pace of industrialisation, laying the foundation for more systemic integration of production structures across national boundaries. However, the overall economic performance in the majority of developing countries has been marked by sluggish growth. The debt-burden and other fiscal difficulties have combined to lower the levels of regional and interregional trade and investment among countries of the South.

Globalisation establishes a new context and a new rationale to expand collective self-reliance in the South through South-South markets in goods, services, and capital. The promising prospects for a South-South market is discernible in the current demographic projections which indicate that by 2025, nearly 7 billion of the projected world population of 8.5 billion will be inhabitants of the South. Taking advantage of these positive projections requires proactive policy initiatives to lay the basic infrastructure and to harmonise norms and standards among trading partners in the South. This will also require negotiating South-South agreements on such subjects as services, investment, intellectual property rights, environmental and labour standards, competition policy, and dispute-settlement mechanisms.

In the financial sector, the South could draw lessons from the crises in Latin America during the 1980s and the recent crisis in Asia in the 1990s as a basis for closer collaboration in establishing prudential regulatory frameworks to ensure well-regulated banking systems and efficient capital markets. Given the shortage of expertise in most developing countries, the integration of Southern countries into the globalising economy will largely depend on political will and institutional mechanisms to promote the sharing of expertise, information, joint training programmes, joint commissioning of technical studies, and the pooling of expertise to negotiate and help government implement viable programmes.

Conclusion

The last four decades have witnessed increasing differentiation among the large group of countries designated as developing countries. Indeed, a few of them are almost fully integrated into the globalised economy. Most of them, however, are still marginal players. To be effective participants, these countries need to understand fully the new opportunities globalisation offers and the new constraints it imposes on the development process.

The first issue addressed here is that globalisation seems to make the idea of development redundant. It would appear that, by the logic of marketisation, development and development co-operation is anachronistic. But it would be self-defeating in the long run if the values of equity, fairness and civilised behaviour are sacrificed on the altar of globalisation.

The second issue relates to the relative autonomy of the developing country state. Globalisation threatens the discretion of the state everywhere. But the more developed the country, the more robust is the response-mechanism of the state. For the developing country, the challenge is to be able to retain the idea of an activist state even while recognising that the new activism must be different from the *dirigisme* of the 1960s and 1970s. The challenge for the international community is to recognise that development requires an exceptional combination of circumstances and to provide the space for each developing country to accommodate its own exceptional circumstances.

The third issue concerns the new urgency for South-South co-operation. The dizzying force of globalisation demands great discipline on the part of policy-makers in the South in establishing the institutional mechanisms and policy processes for a more coherent collaborative framework among developing countries.

References

The literature on globalisation and related issues is quite extensive and growing. The following sources were useful for information and analysis in preparing this article:

Cable, Vincent, 'The Diminished Nation-State: A Study in the Loss of Economic Power', *Daedalus*, Vol. 124, No, 2, 1995

Dunning, H. John, 'The Advent of Alliance Capitalism' in Dunning, John and K.A. Hamdani, eds., *The New Globalism and Developing Countries* (New York: United Nations Press, 1997)

International Monetary Fund, *World Economic Outlook* (Washington D.C.: October, 1997, May 1998)

Rodrik, Dani, *Has Globalisation Gone Too Far?* (Washington, D.C.: Institute for International Economics, 1997)

UNCTAD, *World Investment Reports*, 1995, 1996, 1997

World Bank, *Global Finance* (Washington D.C., 1998)

5

The Recent Systemic Crisis and The Management of The International Financial System
A Latin American Perspective

Introduction

The development, pace, and implications of the most recent systemic crisis, which originated in the Asia region in July 1997, are still unfolding in many Latin American countries. The good macroeconomic performance of 1996 and 1997, which represented a surprisingly quick recovery after the 'tequila' crisis of 1995, will now be compared with the recession which began in 1998 throughout the region. The impact of the Asian crisis in Latin America demonstrates that we are faced with an important systemic crisis, deeper and larger than all the 'post-Bretton Woods' crises.

The lessons to be drawn from the behaviour of the international economic system in the last two years are important not only for domestic policies as such but also for global policies. More than the national dimension, the international ramifications of the crisis lead to an inevitable discussion of the management of the global financial system and of the way to tackle development issues. As Gerry Helleiner noted recently,

'financial instability, banking system failures, exchange rates crises and consequent real macroeconomic disruption have increasingly been seen as a major and, in many cases, a new threat to the development prospects of poor countries. Highest priority has in recent years been reassigned by international development institutions from advice on project evaluation and 'development strategy' which, in any case, often remains controversial, towards macroeconomic and financial sector policy reforms. Moreover, the potential problems created by contagion of financial distress are now seen as threatening to whole regions, and indeed well beyond.' [1]

The vulnerability of Latin American countries and many other developing and 'emerging' economies around the world can not be treated as a limited regional problem. Globalisation transfers the local vulnerabilities to the global level. Based on their own painful experience, the Latin American countries can contribute to the debate with their own analysis of the mechanics of current systemic crises, as well as with their own views on the changes needed in the management of the international monetary and financial system.

This presentation is not intended to provide a complete picture of the Latin American perspective on this topic. It is aimed more at provoking some reflection and additional research, because this new kind of crisis, which may be 'the first of the twenty-first century', [2] needs a serious strategic response, based on a careful assessment of the political and development needs of the region. In this sense, this article will focus on the analysis of the issues more than on solutions and offer partial descriptions rather than prescriptions.

The Impact of the Asian Crisis in Latin America

Following a pattern which was already visible during the Mexican crisis of 1994–95, the impact of the crisis which originated in Thailand in July 1997 on the Latin American economies unfolds in three main stages. First, the monetary impact (on the exchange rates) and the financial impact (on investment flows) are seen in the short-term, immediately after the collapse of the Asian financial policies and which affects access to capital markets. Second, the impact on trade flows, becomes evident only in the medium-term, i.e. six to eight months after the first stage. Finally, the third stage is the one related to the recession in the aftermath of the crisis, which evolves like a deeper wave, with a more perverse but slower impact.

Each one of these stages deserves to be understood as part of an apparently irreversible sequence of events. They all demonstrate the vulnerability of the Latin American region *vis-à-vis* a crisis for which it bears no responsibility. Each stage underlines the systemic features of the Asian crisis.

The First Stage: The Impact on the Access to International Capital Markets

The days and weeks following the devaluation of the Thai currency, the baht, were a period of panic among the new actors in the international financial system. The 'institutional investors' and the 'money managers' who were relying on the high and quick rentability of the emerging economies started a general retreat, looking for more stable destinations, particularly in the case of short-term financial operations. The 'flight to quality' became a global behaviour pattern among investors all over the world in the last quarter of 1997. It continued during the following months, particularly affecting the Latin American countries because they suffered not only from the impact of being compared unfairly to the Asian victims, but also, in August 1998, as a result of the impact of the Russian crisis.

The 'flight to quality' is a crisis of confidence with unpredictable consequences for the capacity of all emerging economies to maintain their credibility in international capital markets. In other words, all emerging economies are viewed in the same way, in spite of their objective differences. Consequently, the good Latin American macroeconomic performance in the aftermath of the 'tequíla' crisis was not sufficient to compensate for the fear of contagion in the region which, fed by fear itself, in fact occurred in a typically vicious circle.

The Latin American stock exchanges were 'contaminated' by this general movement as early as September 1997. The exchange rates trembled, and the spreads of many Latin American bonds, but mainly those of the two key economies of the region, namely Brazil and Argentina, soared while the risk assessment by the rating agencies also deteriorated. Nowadays, the systemic impact of the new financial crises for the 'emerging economies' can be clearly assessed through these two indicators: the spreads of the debt bonds and the agencies' rating determining the flow of international investments. In fact, as was observed in the region during 1998, the contagion affects both short-term and long-term capital (i.e. foreign direct investments). In addition to the contagion effect, the retreat of some Asian investments in the region and the suspension of some new projects which were being prepared (including a number of Japanese investments), can be explained by the lack of liquidity in the Asian banking system after the crisis.

Taken together, these macroeconomic elements constitute the 'configuration risk' of Latin American economies, established during the first stage of the impact by the international capital markets before any official

reaction by the affected governments and by multilateral financial institutions such as the IMF. The time factor appears to be the most important
driving force explaining the behaviour of the main actors during this stage:
the accelerated pace of the contagion, facilitated by the new electronic
devices, is now counted in terms of days or even hours. It is worthwhile to
remember that in 1929, the financial collapse of Wall Street also had large
ramifications in many European stock markets and banking systems, but
at that time, the contagion was measured in months and even years.

The Second Stage: The Medium-term Impact on Trade Flows

The impact on the trade flows may not appear as impressive as the impact
on the exchange rate or the flow of capital, because it evolves only slowly
and does not feature in the news headline. However, from the point of view
of Latin American strategies of development, the second stage may be even
more negative than the first, because it has perverse implications for the
region's productive capacity, its competitiveness in global markets, and
therefore its rates of growth and employment. Since 1997, even before, but
more severely after, the Asian crisis, the main Latin American exports (raw
materials, agricultural commodities, and oil) were affected by four negative
factors in the international markets:

1)   The fall of international commodity prices, involving significant losses
     in earnings, particularly for Peru, Colombia, Chile and Venezuela. This
     decline, which is part of a trend initiated in the 1980s, increased in the
     second half of 1997.

2)   The fall of Asian demand for Latin American exports, affecting more
     specifically Peru and Chile, whose shares of export to Asia represented,
     in 1997, 38.1 per cent and 25.3 per cent, respectively, of their total
     exports.[3]

3)   The increased competitiveness of Asian products in the international
     and regional markets, due to the devaluation of Asian currencies,
     implying that 57.8 per cent of Latin American exports to OECD coun-
     tries face a new Asian competition.[4]

4)   The decreasing global demand for commodities as the world economy
     enters a recession.

Consequently, as stated by the United States Secretary of Commerce, W.
Daley, 'the 1998 global financial crisis may be a global commercial crisis in
1999'. Obviously, the impact on the Latin American trade flows became

The Impact of the Asian Crisis on Latin American Trade and the External Financing Situation

Latin America: global commercial performance
(in millions of dollars)

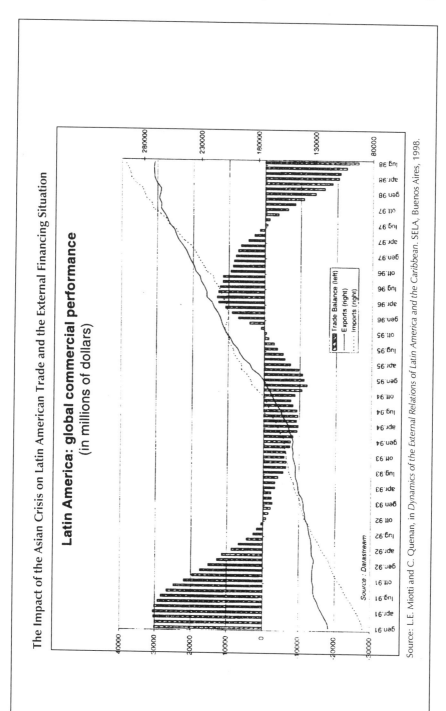

Source : Datastream

Source: L.E. Miotti and C. Quenan, in *Dynamics of the External Relations of Latin America and the Caribbean*. SELA, Buenos Aires, 1998.

more sensitive at the end of 1998, as a consequence of the Brazilian financial crisis and in January 1999, with the devaluation of the Brazilian real. In fact, the direct and indirect impact of the Asian crisis in Latin America in the medium term also includes: 1) the Brazilian monetary and financial crisis which started one year later; 2) the changes caused by devaluation on interregional trade flows; and 3) its paralysing effect on MERCOSUR. The following graph illustrates the external trade and financing situation of the region, the increasing trade deficit and, more importantly, the increasing financing gap which could be aggravated if the access to international capital markets is not soon improved.

The previous graph identifies the general context in which the impact of the Asian crisis in Latin America should be seen. It illustrates the background of the external trade and financing deficit, which looks like a trend started in 1992, in spite of a temporary and limited improvement in the situation from 1996–97.

The graph also confirms one of the conclusions of the UNCTAD *Trade and Development Report*, 1998:

> Since the debt crisis of the 1980s the major challenge in Latin America has been to reconcile growth fast enough to keep unemployment at acceptable levels and reduce poverty with a sustainable external payments position. The recovery that has taken place since the Mexican crisis suggests that this dilemma is still present, as the payments position has continued to worsen, although the deficits now involve a higher proportion of capital goods in total imports than in the past. These difficulties have been compounded by the impact of the East Asian crisis on commodity and petroleum prices. The heavy reliance on private capital inflows to finance the growing payments deficits has meant that Latin American countries are still subject to the risk of contagion.'[5]

The Third Stage: The Recession

In 1998 the financial impact of the Asian crisis, as well as the beginning of the medium-term impact on trade flows, produced a drop of more than 2 per cent in the average GDP growth rate of the region which, however, did not exceed 2.6 per cent (ECLAC estimates). Without the impact of the crisis, the Latin American countries would probably have achieved an average GDP growth rate of 5 per cent or more, which would have been similar to the rates attained in 1996 and 1997. The forecasts for 1999, made by ECLAC and the World Bank at the end of 1998 – which did not include the assessment of the impact of the recent Brazilian 'samba' effect – indicated a regional average growth rate of 1.5 per cent, with deeper recessions in

Brazil and Venezuela. In addition to the economic significance of these figures, it is worthwhile to note that, according to the World Bank, Latin America needs a sustained annual growth of 5 per cent during the next ten years in order to put an end to the increasing rate of poverty.

The impact of the Asian crisis, in terms of growth rates, for Latin American economies should be analysed in the larger context of the global economic recession that affected some of their main trade and investment partners, such as Japan and the European Union.

The Lessons of the Systemic Crises

From the Latin American perspective, the Asian crisis, the 'tequila' effect in 1995, the Russian default in 1998 and the recent 'samba' impact, demonstrate that systemic crises have three main characteristics:

- All the 'emerging economies' are perceived as similar in the international capital markets because of the 'flight to quality'. Michel Camdessus, the former IMF Managing Director, deplored the 'unfair punishment' of the Latin American economies since the impact they suffered was a consequence of problems occurring in other countries or regions.
- The new systemic crises affect all kinds of investment flows, because they generate a sudden retreat of short-term (portfolio) investments from the emerging economies, and they induce a climate of regional and global recession which causes delays or suspension of long-term (direct) investments.
- They have implications for the trade flows, by introducing changes in the traditional trends, by modifying the established positions in traditional markets, and accelerating the impact of decreasing commodity prices, thus aggravating the deterioration of the terms of trade for developing countries. The long-term national and foreign investment flows linked to trade flows are also modified. The slow-down in the plans and programmes of the integration schemes such as MERCOSUR and the Andean Community has to be considered in this context.

An analysis of the systemic crises indicates that Latin America shares the affliction of all 'emerging economies': vulnerability which is due not only to its 'openness' but its hypersensitivity to international contagion.

This vulnerability is aggravated by inappropriate domestic macroeconomic policy choices of the developing countries' such as:

- Financial openness with weak banking supervision (which was one of the main causes of both the Mexican and the Asian crises)

- Mismanagement of the economic 'bonanzas' (which may be one of the roots of the collapse of the Southeast Asian economies')
- Speculative investments and/or short-term foreign capital inflows together with an absence of productive investments (which were factors present in the Mexican and Asian cases)
- Deteriorating terms of trade (particularly obvious in the Latin American economies)
- Unsustainable monetary policies (as was demonstrated in the Mexican and the Brazilian situation)
- Fiscal deficit (a common feature of Latin American countries)

The Lessons for the Management of the International Monetary and Financial System

The extent of the systemic crises and their ramifications for short-term and long-term monetary, financial and commercial flows, has imposed high costs on the international system. The costs are too high to conclude that these crises are similar to 'growth pains' linked to the evolution of the globalisation process. Inertia and improvisation cannot continue to be the only reactions to turmoil too deep and far-reaching to be considered as mere transitional episodes. The realistic possibility that the international system may have to face more crises of this nature in the future emphasises the need to examine critically the management of the system in order to determine what can be done to prevent or to minimise the contagion effect.

The debate on the reform of the Bretton Woods system is one of the main topics in the current multilateral agenda. This paper cannot analyse all of the details of this issue, but the following comments are intended to highlight the main concerns raised by the recent systemic crises, specifically from the Latin American perspective. Four lessons seem to be particularly relevant in this framework.

The first lesson concerns the objectives and the role of the IMF. In the Mexican as well as the Asian crises, the IMF did not comply with its original and fundamental function of 'watchdog' of the international monetary system, since it did not act as an early warning system. Its access to information on the domestic macroeconomic situation and its traditional role in the financial markets were not sufficient to allow the institution to provide adequate warning and thus prevent the collapse of the 'successful' Asian economies and the global contagion which followed in its wake. The globalisation of monetary and financial flows, the increasing role of new actors outside the sphere of governments, and the interdependence of national macroeconomic policies, all call for an early warning mechanism more effective than the kind of supervision currently applied by the IMF in the developing countries.

The second lesson relates to the 'unfairness' of the systemic crises. The major impact of the Asian events on the Latin American countries and many other emerging or transition economies has to be compared with the relatively limited costs borne by the industrialised countries. The vulnerability and hypersensitivity *vis-à-vis* systemic contagion is obviously different and greatly reduced in the case of industrialised countries. The multiplier and perverse effect of the crises on decreasing investment flows is virtually absent for those countries, since they do not rely on external financing. The impact on trade flows certainly has an effect on their economic performance. But even in the worst scenarios, the aggregate loss is measured in terms of 1 or 2 per cent of GDP growth while, for the developing countries, the cost of commercial and financial turmoil could easily involve 7 or 8 per cent of GDP growth.

Thirdly, the systemic crises underline the unsolved problem of development financing. Access to the international capital markets (which has played a decisive role in all the recent crises, much more than the need to complement internal savings) is a vital element of long-term development strategies. The terms of the debate on development financing may have changed since the external debt crisis of the 1980s, but the essence of the issue is still the same, particularly for the Latin American countries. Any review of the management of the monetary and financial system must therefore address the issue of guaranteed access by the developing countries to stable and productive investments for their long-term development.

Finally, as far as the structure of the Bretton Woods institutions is concerned, it seems that the concept of the 'triangle' (trade, monetary, and financial policies) established in 1944 is still basically valid. The interdisciplinary aspects of the globalisation process require an integrated approach, linking domestic and international economic policies. The impact of the contagion effect in the monetary, financial and commercial areas is evidence that the 'triangle' is a concept that reflects current international economic reality as it did more than fifty years ago when the system was designed. However, the current institutional framework of the WTO, the IMF, and the World Bank would need to be updated in order to respond to the changes generated by globalisation. In revisiting these institutions, the need for an effective early warning mechanism and a sustainable development financing capability, together with the establishment of an effective link with trade are probably the main priorities to be addressed. As Helleiner has remarked:

> these 'new' financial issues have by now assumed such regional, and even potential global, importance that any negotiation of longer-term development or trade co-operation cannot be credible without full provision for co-operation in financial crisis prevention and management within a fully integrated trade-financial co-operation package. It is no longer plausible for some intergovernmental agencies to address purely trade issues (sometimes even trade in financial services) in one forum while totally different ones (often considerably more powerful) 'sort out' the financial issues separately in another.[6]

Some Conclusions

The economic and political dimensions of the mismanagement of the international monetary and financial system, and the risks raised by the various crises, point to the need for 'good governance' of the system. The notion of governance as applied at the domestic level involves political and ethical values such as participation, transparency, equity, and stability.

Taking into account these basic values, and by extrapolating the notion of governance to the international economic system, the issue of 'global economic governance' should be put on the multilateral agenda. This would mean that:

- Any attempt to revise the rules and the functioning of the institutional mechanisms governing the current financial and monetary system that does not include the issue of the development financing, and that is limited in terms of its ability to tackle the volatility of capital flows, is inefficient *a priori*, as far as the developing countries are concerned.
- Any effort by the international financial institutions to tackle the issue of the management of the system without a strong and broad international political consensus will produce only ephemeral results.

There are many obstacles in the way of ensuring a meaningful discussion on global economic governance. First, there is the usual tendency to divide the international economic agenda into many specific issues and to pursue discussions on them in different fora. This is why, for example, it is easier to talk about banking supervision than to consider the broader and more sensitive issue of the quality of foreign investments.

Second, the increasing proliferation of actors (institutional investors, money managers, governments, international and regional financial institutions, etc.), where both governmental and non-governmental entities play a role in the system, does not help the decision-making process or the formulation of rules of the game that are equitable for all.

Third, the debate on the redesign of the current international financial and monetary architecture may have just started and is probably heading down a tortuous road. As a recent article in *The Economist* stated,

> listing the problems may be easy; finding solutions is not. Should there be more or less global regulation, more or less public financial support, looser or tighter exchange rate regimes? There are no simple answers, because the problems of modern economic policy are maddeningly inter-linked. A policy-maker trying to design the ideal financial system has three objectives. He wants continuing national sovereignty: financial markets that are regulated, supervised and cushioned; and the benefits of global capital markets. Unfortunately (. . .) these three goals are incompatible. They form the 'impossible trinity' that underlies the instability of today's global architecture.[7]

The fourth obstacle is related to the political forces needed to introduce new mechanisms and new criteria for the management of the international system. The main driving force, as was the case in the establishment the Bretton Woods institutions, is political leadership. Neither the United States, nor the European Union, nor Japan nor, unfortunately, the developing countries, acting in isolation have the political leadership required for this purpose. New alliances will therefore have to be forged to change the way in which systemic crises and the impact of the globalisation process are dealt with at the international level. It is quite possible that the threat of a generalised crisis, worse than those witnessed in the past, may provide the incentive to begin a meaningful process of transformation of the mechanisms for managing the global economic system. The articulation of clear and viable solutions nevertheless constitutes a fundamental requirement for adapting and reforming the global financial system in order to enable it to function in an equitable and efficient manner.

Notes

1. Gerry Helleiner, 'Financial Markets, Crises and Contagion: Issues for Smaller Countries in the FTAA and Post-Lomé IV Negotiations'; paper prepared for the Caribbean Regional Negotiating Machinery, Kingston, Jamaica, January 1999, p.1

2. The term was first used by Michel Camdessus, former Managing Director of the International Monetary Fund, referring to the Mexican crisis of 1994–95

3. See SELA, *The Impact of the Asian Crisis on Latin America* (Caracas, February 1998)

4. R.E. Saez, 'Latin American Exporters to the OECD markets potentially more exposed to the Asian Crisis: a First Look' (Washington D.C.: Inter-American Development Bank, March 1998, mimeo)

5. UNCTAD, *Trade and Development Report*, 1998 (Geneva: United Nations, 1999, p.14)

6. Gerry Helleiner, op.cit., p.1

7. *The Economist, Global Financial Survey*, 'Time for a Redesign?', January 30, 1999, p.4

6

Globalisation and Counter-Globalisation

The Caribbean in the Context of the South

N O R M A N   G I R V A N

Process and Ideology

Let us begin by distinguishing 'globalisation' as an ideological term associated with a concrete project of the 1990s, from globalisation as a substantive process. Insofar as the construction of a capitalist world economy is an historical process that commenced with European maritime and commercial expansion towards the end of the fifteenth century, it can be said that globalisation in the substantive sense has been taking place over the past 500 years. The 'South', as it is known today, was brought into being by this process.

Over the course of this history a succession of labels has been applied to the specific projects characteristic of a given period. Thus there have been 'Mercantilism', 'Free Trade', 'Imperialism', 'The White Man's Burden', 'The Pax Brittanica', 'Development' and the 'Cold War'. A label sums up the concrete system of power relations, rules of the game, institutions, practices, and policies established for a particular period. A label also conveys an ideology, that is, a set of assumptions about the way the world works and ought to work, which may be codified as a theory with claims to scientific status. Ideological use of a label provides legitimacy for the project by asserting that it is inevitable and to everyone's benefit.

'Globalisation' in its ideological usage is the label employed for the post-Cold War, US-led project of the 1990s to organise the world according to the principles of neo-liberal economics. It connotes an allegedly irreversible process towards the formation of a single world economy, society, and culture driven by technology and by the transnationalisation of investment and of money capital. Reduction and eventual elimination of barriers to the movement of goods, services, and capital across national borders is held to be at once inevitable, necessary, and universally benign. It can be further broken down into: 1) the set of market-oriented practices that governments are required to adopt; 2) the multilateral institutions responsible for policing and enforcing these practices; and 3) the legitimising theory and ideology, that is, neo-liberalism.

Context

The immediate antecedents of the project were the turbulent events of the previous two decades. The abandonment of the Bretton Woods system at the beginning of the 1970s was to have major long-term consequences, for it established a framework in which currency speculation and its offshoots became major sources of profit for international finance. The OPEC price increases of 1973 further fuelled the growth of the Eurodollar market, which found profitable opportunities for international lending to both surplus- and deficit-developing countries. Hence the external debt of the South grew rapidly and, together with a decline in commodity prices in the second half of the 1970s, led to a sharp deterioration in its bargaining power towards the end of the decade. Accordingly, militant demands for the establishment of an NIEO, based on the principles of equity and justice, faded into the background.

The beginning of the 1980s saw the Keynesian consensus in the North replaced by the new orthodoxy of neo-liberal monetarism, reflected in the Thatcher/Reagan administrations in Britain and the United States. The subsequent interest-rate shocks imposed in the US and elsewhere in the name of a monetarist anti-inflation strategy threw the South into a severe debt crisis that started in Mexico in 1982 and continued throughout the 1980s. It provided the lever by which the Northern-dominated international financial institutions were able to impose severe neo-liberal policy conditionalities on much of the South. The measures centred on devaluation, privatisation, and trade and investment liberalisation. Financing for structural adjustment and policy reform replaced financing for development.

By 1986 the South was in full retreat. UNCTAD was now to be eclipsed by GATT as the main forum for international trade negotiations. The agenda shifted from effecting structural reforms in the international trading system for the promotion of development, to lowering barriers to trade and investment for the promotion of market-led growth. The growth in new information and communications technologies also led to the determined – and successful – bid by the US to include services and intellectual property in the Uruguay Round of the GATT negotiations. Conclusion of the Uruguay Round saw the establishment of a new global institution, the WTO, with wide-ranging treaty powers to enforce the rules of the open international trading regime.

At the same time, each of the three capitalist centres intensified efforts to strengthen its position *vis-à-vis* the other two by the formation of economic zones. The European Community made plans to transform itself in to the European Union. Japan continued to consolidate itself as the centre of an Asia-Pacific economic zone; while the United States initiated talks for the creation of the North American Free Trade Agreement (NAFTA), which would lead to the FTAA project of the 1990s.

The collapse of Eastern European socialism and the USSR provided the catalyst for the conversion of trade and financial liberalisation into a truly global project. The remaining non-capitalist economies, led by China, were already adopting market-oriented reforms and opening up to direct foreign investment. They were to accept many, though not all, of the practices of the new orthodoxy.

The Globalisation Project of the 1990s

The globalisation project of the 1990s was based on a coherent political, institutional, theoretical, and ideological order; and had a set of prescribed practices and a convenient and easily-recognised label. We see *ten* features as central:

(1) A world economic order centred on the Triad of US-EU-Japan, under the political and military leadership of the US
(2) The central role of the WTO in international trade relations
(3) The construction of regional economic blocs or free trade zones
(4) Restructuring North-South trade agreements (NAFTA, FTAA, Lomé) along WTO- compatible lines; that is, replacement of the principle of non-reciprocal preferences to assist the development of weaker partners with that of reciprocal trade liberalisation to promote trade expansion and market-led growth

(5) Policies of privatisation, financial deregulation, trade and exchange rate liberalisation, fiscal and monetary orthodoxy, labour market reform, and social welfare reform, as the new orthodoxy with presumed universal applicability

(6) The alleged loss of national economic sovereignty flowing from the imperative for all governments to adopt standard neo-liberal measures in order to maintain competitiveness and attract investment capital

(7) The attainment of 'global competitiveness' as the benchmark by which all countries and producers, regardless of their resources or level of development, are to be evaluated through participation in the global market place (the 'level playing field')

(8) The growth of global telecommunications – computer networks, satellite TV, and the Internet – as the technological infrastructure in the globalisation of finance, production, marketing, and patterns of consumption

(9) The consolidation of huge concentrations of private capital – transnational corporations and institutional investors – as the dominant players in world production, trade, and finance

(10) A triumphalist ideology, marked by the assumption that there is no other way to organise the world, as summed up in the phrase 'the end of history'

However, the global financial crisis which emerged in 1997 will probably prove to be a turning point. As a result of its devastating economic and social consequences over large parts of the world, the political, theoretical, and ideological basis of the globalisation project has been seriously undermined. We now see clear signs of the emergence of 'counter-globalisation' as a distinct tendency of the next decade.

Counter-Globalisation

We may use the term counter-globalisation to refer to critiques of market-oriented, corporate-led globalisation and to social movements that advocate alternative ways of managing national and international exchange.[1] Counter-globalisation does not necessarily imply a retreat to a world of autarchic national entities – though some elements do advocate a 'return to the local' (Mander and Goldsmith, 1998). Rather it questions the assumption that global market liberalisation will work to the benefit of all, inducing weaker economies to become more competitive, generating equitable all-round economic growth and leading to desirable social and environmental outcomes with minimum government intervention and no need for social management. This assumption is contradicted by the fact that international markets are skewed against the poorer countries of the world, by the evidence on widening income inequalities among nations, and by the rapid pace of environmental degradation. In the words of the UNDP's Human Development Report for 1997:

> Globalisation is . . . proceeding apace, but largely for the benefit of the more dynamic and powerful countries of the North and the South. The loss to developing countries from unequal access to trade, labour and finance (is) estimated . . . at $500 billion a year, 10 times what they receive annually in foreign assistance. (Human Development Report, 1997: 87)

Among the findings highlighted in this and other issues of the Human Development Reports are:

- In international financial markets, real interest rates are 4 times higher for poor countries than for rich countries. Eighty-three per cent of foreign direct investment goes to rich countries, and three-quarters of the remainder goes to ten developing countries, mostly in East and Southeast Asia and in Latin America. The countries with the poorest 20 per cent of the world's people receive just 0.2 per cent of international commercial lending. (HDR, 1992: 48; 1996: 9)
- Developed countries impose the highest trade barriers on goods in which developing countries have the greatest competitive advantage: textiles, clothing and footwear. The cost to the developing countries of these barriers has been estimated by the IMF at $50 billion a year. (HDR, 1994: 66)
- Domestic agricultural subsidies and price supports by the industrial countries cost the developing and formerly centrally-planned economies approximately $22 billion a year in foregone export revenues (HDR, 1992: 48; HDR 1994: 67)
- Cumulative terms-of-trade losses by the developing countries amounted to $290 billion between 1980 and 1991. (HDR, 1997: 84)
- The share in world trade of the world's poorest countries, with 20 per cent of the world's people, has declined from 4 per cent to less than 1 per cent from 1960 to 1990. (HDR, 1996: 9)
- Although the net benefits from the GATT Uruguay Round agreements are estimated at $212–$510 billion per year, the losses will be concentrated among countries that are least able to afford them: sub-Saharan Africa will lose up to $1.2 billion per year, and the least developed countries $600 million. (HDR, 1997: 82)
- The poorest 20 per cent of the world's people saw their share in world income decline from 2.3 per cent to 1.4 per cent in the past three decades;

while that of the richest 20 per cent grew from 70 to 85 per cent. The ratio of the shares grew from 30:1 to 61:1.(HDR, 1996:8)

- The assets of the world's 358 billionaires exceed the combined annual incomes of the 2.5 billion people who comprise the poorest 45 per cent of mankind. (HDR 1996:8)
- Global warming has already become a serious problem; twenty countries already suffer from water stress; a sixth of the world's land area is now degraded; deforestation has reduced the wooded area per 1,000 inhabitants by 36 per cent since 1970; world fish stocks are declining; and wild species are becoming extinct at 50–100 times the natural rate. (HDR 1998:4)

Counter-globalisation challenges the neo-liberal assumption that markets are 'free and fair' and lead to optimal outcomes, which is the theoretical underpinning of global and regional trade liberalisation. This implies that the subjects of market information, market transparency, market regulation and market structure reform are relevant areas for international negotiation. Similarly, the principle of gradated differentiation of treatment of countries and groups of countries according to their ability to compete effectively in an open trading environment should be retained and reinforced as in integral part of international trade arrangements.

A basic question is, 'What is the ultimate objective of the achievement of "global competitiveness" at the national level and by what means is such competitiveness to be achieved?' Competitiveness achieved at the cost of increasing unemployment, social exclusion, poverty and inequality is not acceptable. Heightened efficiency that results from equipping the poor and marginalised with education, skills, health care, and economic assets is to be welcomed. Global markets should be supportive of poverty reduction and human development, rather than sacrificing the latter to the needs of the former. Instead of blanket trade liberalisation there would be selectivity and sequencing of trade liberalisation, complemented by strategies to build up technological and managerial capabilities among producers at the micro-level and to empower the poor and the marginalised.

Theoretically, this approach questions the universalism implicit in the neo-liberal paradigm. According to this approach, all economies obey certain universal laws of economics and correspondingly the policies that guarantee economic success are essentially the same in every country. Epistemologically, universalism is rooted in the claims of neo-classical economics to be akin to the natural sciences, especially physics. The opposing view, which is associated with institutional economics, is that economic processes are embedded in specific social contexts. The world community exhibits wide diversity in history, institutions, culture, social and economic structure, and politics. Hence the functioning of markets, the nature of entrepreneurship, and the capacity of the state machinery varies from country to country.

Accordingly, questions related to the role of 'market vs. state' cannot be determined outside a specific context in time and place. Each country will need to find the combination of mechanisms – state vs. market; and organisation – state, private sector, small enterprises, co-operatives, or community organisations – that works best, given its historical legacy and its specific economic, social, institutional, and cultural setting. What succeeds in one country may fail in another, and vice versa. This is more so when issues of social and human development, equity, and ecological sustainability are to be addressed, for these require the inclusion of civil society in governance and economic management.

To work out a suitable blend of market, state and civil society in economic management, countries need to have room for experimentation and social learning in a supportive global environment. Universalistic neo-liberalism therefore should be replaced with respect for diversity and acceptance of the principles of pluralism, particularity, and learning. Balancing this against the need for a minimum set of standards and rules to govern international economic exchange is a matter for international negotiation.

Counter-globalisation therefore questions the theory, the ideology, and the practices of neo-liberal globalisation. It draws on a wide range of social forces: governments of disadvantaged countries in the South; labour unions in the North which fear the loss of jobs to low-wage locations in the South; protectionist lobbies in the North; environmental groups; and community organisations. A major factor is the emergence of North-South counter-globalisation coalitions of citizen's groups and other NGOs. Here we may speak of 'the globalisation of counter-globalisation'.

In general these organisations advocate an alternative order based on the principles of equity, social justice, democratic participatory governance, and ecological sustainability. This should apply both within and among nations. However, counter-globalisation is not necessarily a united, coherent body of opinion and political action. There are contradictions among NGOs and between NGOs, governments, and labour unions. This produces a pattern of 'shifting coalitions' around specific issues, e.g. the MAI, NAFTA, the IMF, and the Convention on Global Climate Change. It represents so far a kind of global social movement in the making. But it has considerable potential for the future, given the global scope of the problems of poverty, the subordination of women, and ecological degradation; and given the powerful tools available to the movement from global communications technologies. All the signs are that this movement will have a growing impact, *vis-à-vis* the state system both in the North and South, on shaping the form and content of globalisation.

The World Financial Crisis and Globalisation

The world financial crisis of 1997–99 was a turning point in the globalisation project. A principal tenet of the project – capital-account liberalisation and the deregulation of financial systems – has been largely discredited. There is broad agreement that the crisis was largely the result of the unrestricted, unregulated and unmonitored inflow of short-term capital to the affected countries followed by abrupt and massive capital flight that often had little to do with underlying conditions in particular countries ('contagion of emerging markets' effect). Prominent establishment economists are now conceding the necessity for government regulation of financial systems and more generally in the market economy, notably Stiglitz (1998). This is manifested in the variety of positions adopted on desirable reforms of the 'global financial architecture' (Box 6.I). The absence of a clear consensus on this question so far is a reflection of contradictory interests among the US, the EU, and Japan; and also between finance capital, industrial capital, and among different factions of finance capital.

One possible outcome of this process is for the extreme market-oriented version of globalisation to be shaded into one that recognises a role for

---

BOX 6.1

Reform of the International Monetary/Financial System: Some positions

1. Greater information, transparency, monitoring and surveillance of short-term flows; strengthening of IMF role; reform of domestic regulatory systems in developing countries
   Supported by the US, the IMF and the World Bank
2. IMF should become lender of last resort
   Proposed by Stanley Fischer, chief economist at the IMF
3. IMF should become world Central Bank
   Proposed by George Soros
4. US Federal Reserve could become international lender of last resort
   Proposed by Joint Economic Committee of US Congress
5. Controls on short-term capital flows by recipient countries
   Proposed by UNCTAD, leading voices in the EU, and Japan; already adopted by some Asian developing countries

global financial regulation. This might work against the immediate interests of finance/speculative capital, but it could be supportive of the continued globalisation of production and long-term investment by providing a more stable global economic environment. We might call this scenario a regime of 'globally managed neo-liberalism'.

The very fluidity of the current process, due to the existence of contradictory interests within the Triad, should be seen as providing a window of opportunity for the South. So far the voice of the South has hardly been heard on the issues of reform of the international monetary and financial system and there is an urgent need for these countries to insert themselves more vigorously into this debate with proposals of their own.

There is also the question of the impact on the globalisation project of the long-term social and political changes triggered by the crisis. Millions of people have been thrown into poverty and unemployment, unleashing social movements and political forces that blame international finance and its corrupt local allies for their plight. Several countries are now experimenting with unorthodox measures, such as capital controls and limiting foreign access to domestic capital markets. The unravelling of the globalisation consensus could see many countries becoming more nationalistic and statist, providing examples to others. Some countries may draw lessons from the example of China, which had refused to engage in capital-account liberalisation or to float its currency and survived the financial crisis relatively unscathed.

Hence the longer-term effects of the global financial crisis could be either to weaken or to renovate the globalisation project, depending on how effectively the various actors – especially the South – develop strategies to defend and extend their interests.

Position of the South

The South as a cohesive force in international economic relations (G77, NAM) has been in virtual retreat since the tide turned against it in the run-up to the WTO. It has been further fractured through 'regionalisation' of North-South negotiations within the framework of the EU-ACP, NAFTA and the FTAA contexts; as well as by the rapid growth of East Asia followed by its equally dramatic collapse. Another factor undermining cohesion is ideological diversity: many governments in the South are of strongly neo-liberal persuasion and emphasise market liberalisation rather than market structure reform.

The reality is that the South is a far more heterogeneous group of countries than it was 30-40 years ago, when the 'Third World' was conceived. This is so whether the reference point is level of per capita income, dependence on primary commodities, degree of industrial and technological development, incidence of poverty among the population, social and political structures, or ideological orientation. (Size has always been a major point of differentiation.) To the extent that there is a common factor, it lies in the generally (though not uniformly) subordinate relationship of the countries of the South with the capitalist centres in international trade, technology, and finance and in the negotiations governing these processes. In other words 'the South' is defined by the nature of power relations in the international system.

This also calls into question the concept of the 'South' as a cohesive bloc with common interests across a whole range of specific issues, and concerned exclusively with relations on the inter-state level. It may be more realistic to think of a series of coalitions organised around specific common interests shared by particular groups of states and civil society organisations. Already this development is under way at the level of NGOs. At the inter-state level within the South, the realities of differentiation are evident in the existence of the group of Small Island Developing States (SIDS) for the purpose of environmental negotiations, in the grouping of Least Developed Countries (LLDCs), and in associations of primary commodity exporters.

However, global trade negotiations are still structured on the presumed cohesiveness of the South as a group, with the three regional sub-groups of Asia, Africa, and Latin America and the Caribbean. It is not at all clear that this is the most appropriate structure for purposes of negotiation. Each regional sub-group contains countries whose interests are often contradictory. China, India, Brazil, and Indonesia, for instance, are large states with a considerable degree of industrial development. They have much more in common with one another than they do with sub-Saharan Africa, or with the small countries of Latin America and the Caribbean. We could envisage, therefore, a coalition grouping of small states, of large states, of manufacturing exporters, of primary commodity exporters, and of LLDCs. The Caribbean, as a collection of small and mini-states, needs therefore to review its position within the wider setting of the South and the broad currents of the counter-globalisation movement.

Globalisation and the Caribbean

The context in which Caribbean countries have been impacted by globalisation is characterised by:

(1) **Small size:** The 28 entities of the insular Caribbean have an aggregate population of only 36 million; 22 have populations of less than 1 million.

(2) **Dependency:** The trade/GDP ratio averages 112 per cent for 25 Caribbean states and territories. Most countries specialise in a narrow range of goods and/or services exported to a narrow range of metropolitan markets (US, EU, Russia), relying on EU trade preferences in the case of traditional agricultural products. Financial dependency is evident in the degree of foreign financing (commercial and concessional) for government capital expenditure and sometimes for recurrent spending.

(3) **Fragmentation:** Twelve entities are dependent territories of the four colonial powers – Britain, France, the Netherlands and the United States. The independent states comprise English-speaking (12), Spanish-speaking (2), and French- and Dutch-speaking (one each). There is no single integration grouping for the insular Caribbean. The Caribbean Community – Caricom – includes all the English-speaking states and Suriname and has admitted Haiti, but Cuba and the Dominican Republic (DR) are not members. Cariforum comprises Caricom and the DR but excludes Cuba, and is not a true integration grouping since its functions are limited to co-ordinating trade and aid negotiations with the EU. The Association of Caribbean States (ACS) includes all the insular Caribbean plus the littoral states in Central and South America from Mexico to Venezuela, most of which belong to other integration groupings (i.e. NAFTA, SICA, and the Andean System).

Given these characteristics, globalisation has generated strong cross-currents within the region. Differences in production structures and external association have often resulted in contradictory short-term interests among countries and marked divergences in economic policy. There is a growing interest in regional co-operation, but this will need to address the formidable obstacles arising out of the wide economic differentiation among countries and the legacy of political and linguistic fragmentation. Below we discuss this in terms of the issues of policy convergence, external relations, and regional co-operation.

Policy Convergence

All Caribbean states have instituted market-oriented policy reforms of one kind or another in the past two decades. But the changes have varied widely and have resulted in marked policy divergence in some areas of macro-economic policy. Within Caricom this is most evident in exchange-rate policy, where Guyana, Jamaica and Trinidad and Tobago have instituted floating rates and no capital controls whereas Barbados and the ECCB countries have maintained fixed rates with restrictions on capital movements. The DR and Haiti also have floating exchange-rate regimes whereas Cuba follows a two-tier system. There are also differences among countries in the degree of privatisation and of trade and financial liberalisation. In general, the countries with the most severe debt and adjustment crises in the 1980s have gone the farthest in embracing neo-liberal policy reforms (with the notable exception of Cuba). This may constrain the readiness of their governments to adopt a critical stance *vis-à-vis* the underlying principles of globalisation as expressed in external negotiations.

External Relations

The majority of Caribbean countries are unique in the developing world in having enjoyed one-way preferential trading arrangements with both the EU under Lomé and the US under the CBI. Now both of these arrangements are being undercut by the requirements of multilateral, reciprocal trade liberalisation under the terms of the WTO Treaty. (Cuba lost its preferential trade arrangements with the USSR and other CMEA countries after 1989.)

The impact of the WTO is both direct, stemming from the requirements of the WTO Treaty itself, and indirect, due to the efforts to promote 'WTO compatibility' in the renegotiation of the Lomé agreement and in the FTAA negotiations. In fact it is the latter that is posing the most immediate competitive challenges to Cariforum and CBI countries. An additional complicating factor in the negotiations is that Cariforum countries are allied with African and Pacific countries in the ACP Group under Lomé and with Central American countries in the Small Country Group within the FTAA negotiations. There is also the issue of 'cross-compatibility' between the terms of the FTAA and post-Lomé arrangements.

The EU, Lomé and Cariforum

The successful conclusion of the ACP-EU Lomé negotiations in early 2000 represented a generally favourable outcome for the Caribbean and, indeed, the rest of the ACP Group. Not only does the Convention reflect a continued commitment on the part of the EU to provide a reasonably significant level of development assistance, but it has recognised the need to extend preferential arrangements to the region for the duration of the new agreement. Equally significant is the fact that the agreement recognises the unity of the

ACP Group and thus backed away from the concept of Regional Economic Partnership Arrangements (REPA), originally proposed by the EU as a basis for trade liberalisation between the EU and five separate regional groupings falling within the ACP Group, namely, the Caribbean (Caricom, Haiti and the Dominican Republic); CEMAC; the East African Community (EAC); the Pacific Region; and the Southern African Development Community (SADC), which many studies have suggested would have had a negative impact on the majority of regions.[1] Having said this, the REPA concept remains on the table as an option for future ACP/EU relations on the clear understanding that other options would also be open to the ACP countries or regions not wishing to negotiate REPAs and would involve no less favourable terms than those they enjoy under the present Convention. An accommodation was also reached on the issue of good governance, which had been pushed by the EU but strongly opposed by the ACP Group on the ground that it represented an unacceptable form of political conditionality. In the end, both parties in the negotiations agreed to adopt a suitable reference to the need to prevent bribery and corruption as an important aspect of the overall development effort.

From CBI to NAFTA to FTAA

Following the NAFTA of 1994, Mexican and Canadian producers were given duty-free access to the US market. It eroded the preferential advantages which Caribbean Basin exporters had enjoyed under the Caribbean Basin Initiative (CBI) of 1983 and the 806/807 Customs provisions (Gonzales 1995, p. 5–10). Caribbean Basin governments have been pressing Washington for 'NAFTA Parity' – that is, duty-free access to the US market equivalent to that of Mexico and Canada. After some delay, legislation granting such parity was adopted by the US in May 2000. The option of NAFTA accession by Caricom or by some of its member states was also contemplated at the time when the US Administration had 'fast-track' authority to expand NAFTA by means of a series of bilateral negotiations, but this no longer applies. US Administration policy now centres on the promotion of the Free Trade Agreement of the Americas (FTAA) by means of hemisphere-wide negotiations (excepting Cuba) which were launched in 1998 with 2005 as the target date for the conclusion. US policy is that the FTAA should be both NAFTA-consistent and WTO-compatible. The agreement will cover liberalisation of trade in services and of investment flows, and a whole range of regulatory issues involving government policies and practices.

BOX 6.2

FTAA negotiations: structure and principles

The Declaration of San Jose, adopted at the Ministerial Meeting of March 1998 and ratified at the Second Summit of the Americas, outlined the following structure and principles on the FTAA negotiations.

Structure
Negotiations to be the direct responsibility of a Trade Negotiating Committee at Vice-Ministerial level, meeting twice a year. Negotiations to be concluded by January 1, 2005. Final stages will be co-chaired by Brazil and the United States. Nine negotiating groups established on:-

1. Agriculture
2. Market access
3. Investments
4. Services
5. Government procurement
6. Competition policy
7. Dispute settlement
8. Intellectual property rights
9. Subsidies, anti-dumping and countervailing duties

A Consultative Group on Smaller Economies will monitor negotiations and report directly to the Trade Negotiating Committee on matters affecting the interests of smaller economies.

General Principles
1. Decisions will be made by consensus
2. Negotiations will be transparent
3. The agreement will be consistent with the terms of the WTO
4. The agreement will improve on WTO rules and disciplines wherever possible.
5. Negotiations will be simultaneous and will be treated as parts of a single undertaking
6. The FTAA can co-exist with bilateral and sub-regional agreements, where the terms of such agreements are not covered by, or go beyond, the terms of the FTAA
7. Countries may participate individually or as member of a sub-regional integration group negotiating as a unit
8. Special attention to be given to the needs and conditions of smaller economies
9. In various thematic areas, measures such as technical assistance and longer implementation periods may be included to facilitate the adjustment of smaller economies
10. Measures to facilitate smaller economies should be transparent, simple and easily applicable
11. Countries to ensure that their laws, regulations, and procedures conform to the FTAA agreement.
12. Differences in the level of development among countries to be taken into account.

Source: based on FTAA (1998c)

Table 6.1

Major Negotiating Players in the FTAA – Ranked by GDP .

Country/Group	Population		GDP	
	Mill.	% total	$Bill.	% total
1.USA	263.1	35.0	6952.0	76.0
2. Mercosur and Chile	216.1	28.7	1062.0	11.6
3. Canada	29.6	3.9	568.9	6.2
4. Mexico	90.1	12.0	250.0	2.7
5. Andean Community	100.5	13.4	232.6	2.5
6. CACM, Panama, DR	39.4	5.2	58.5	0.6
7. Caricom	13.4	1.8	20.3	0.2
Smaller Economies				
(6+7)	52.8	7.0	78.8	0.9

Source: based on data in *World Bank World Development Report*, 1997 (Ceara Hatton, 1998)

In the run-up to the FTAA negotiations, Caribbean countries had joined forces with Central America in forming the Working Group on Smaller Economies (Report 1997), which grew out of earlier co-operation in lobbying for NAFTA parity. Initially, there were hopes for acceptance of the principle of special treatment for smaller economies as part of the basic negotiating parameters of the FTAA Treaty. Special treatment could mean the granting of one-way, non-reciprocal trade liberalisation to benefit the small economies of Central America and the Caribbean. Failing this, there could be a longer period of adjustment to full liberalisation. The rationale would be their competitive weaknesses due to absence of economies of scale. This principle was not fully accepted by other FTAA participating countries in the preparatory meetings. The Declaration of San Jose includes the principle of 'special attention to the needs and conditions' of smaller economies, to be supported by a consultative group on the terms of the negotiations, and the group had to settle for a consultative group rather than a separate negotiating group.

To take advantage of these modest concessions, Caribbean and Central American countries face a formidable task. They will be required to service nine separate negotiating groups with technical and professional personnel whilst using the consultative group to maximum effect. The limitations in bargaining power are shown by the fact that the smaller economies together have less than 1 per cent of the aggregate GDP of FTAA negotiating countries and only 7 per cent of the combined population. So far, Caricom has been participating as one unit through the Regional Negotiating Machinery (RNM), while the DR and the Central American (SICA) countries have been coordinating their position. The FTAA negotiations have started in slow gear due to the absence of fast-track authority in the US Administration and the effects of the world financial crisis. The devastating effects of Hurricane Mitch have also led some Central American countries to press for duty-free access to the US market as a special concession.

The bigger picture is that Caribbean and Central American countries could be required within 10 years to open their markets in goods, services, and investment to producers from the US, Canada, and the more industrially advanced Latin American countries; and to compete on an equal footing with them in their traditional US market. Cariforum countries are also bound by the obligations of the current Lome arrangements. Should they participate in a final FTAA Treaty, they will be bound to give free trade privileges to the EU as well. The FTAA is important to Caricom for US market access whilst the EU relationship is important for traditional agricultural exports and for concessional aid. Handling both sets of negotiations and the related diplomatic-political relationships (the US, the EU, Central America, and the non-Caricom Caribbean, and the ACP) constitutes a formidable task requiring a high degree of technical preparation and inter-governmental co-ordination.

The current 'banana war' between the US and the EU is a prime example of a number of the issues touched on here. First, it shows how the fate of small economies can be decided by changes in international trading arrangements over which they have virtually no control. Ultimately, this dispute, which affects the livelihoods of thousands of small producers in the mini-states of Dominica, St Vincent, and St Lucia, will be resolved through the negotiation of power relations between the US and the EU. Second, the dispute underscores the new role of the WTO as the institutional mechanism by which the new rules of the open multilateral trading regime are negotiated and enforced. Third, it dramatises the reduced strategic importance and leverage of the small Caribbean states in the post-Cold War era. Fourth, it shows how the policies of a major power (the US) can be made hostage to corporate interests through the perverse operation of its political system. And fifth, it shows how the short-term interests of different groups of developing countries (in this case the Caribbean and Central/South America) can be pitted against one another as a result of the global thrust towards multilateral free trade driven by transnational corporations.

Regional Co-operation

One positive effect of globalisation-induced trade liberalisation has been to stimulate co-operation efforts across traditional linguistic barriers within the Greater Caribbean region. In a sense this was anticipated by the scope of the Caribbean Basin Initiative, which for the first time in history brought together the Caribbean and Central America (Cuba and Nicaragua excepted) within the coverage of a preferential trading arrangement. The 1990s have seen three significant institutional developments in regional co-operation. First, the Lome Convention was expanded to include Haiti and the DR in the ACP group, and these two countries joined with Caricom in forming Cariforum for the purpose of trade and aid negotiations with the EU. Second, the Association of Caribbean States (ACS) was established with membership covering all the independent states of the Greater Caribbean (Caribbean Basin). The ACS is a mechanism of co-operation in trade, transport and tourism. And third, Caricom was expanded to admit its first non-Anglophone members, Suriname and, more recently, Haiti.

To point to the significance of these developments is not to underestimate the obstacles in the way of wider regional co-operation. The membership of the ACS is a highly disparate collection of states in terms of size, per capita income, economic structure, and integration groupings (Table 6.2). The ACS will not negotiate as a unit in the context of the FTAA, since the majority of members already belong to existing integration arrangements, including NAFTA (Mexico), the Central American Integration System, the

Table 6.2.

Greater Caribbean: Population, Land Area, and GDP by Sub-group 1

Group	No.	Pop. Mil	Area 000 km2	GDP Bbl. US$	GDP $US Per. Cap.	Percent Pop.	Area	GDP	PCY Ratio
G3	3	147.8	4025.4	401.2	2713	68.2	76.6	73.1	107
CACM	5	29.5	423.7	39.0	1324	13.6	8.1	7.1	52
CARICOM	14	13.4	464.1	20.3	1511	6.2	8.8	3.7	60
Not grouped*	3	20.8	238.4	31.7	1520	9.6	4.5	5.8	60
Dependent territories	12	5.1	105.2	56.9	11099	2.4	2.0	10.4	438
Total	37	216.7	5256.7	549.0	2533	100.0	100.0	100	100

*Cuba, the Dominican Republic and Panama
Source: Based on Ceara 1997, Annex Table 1

Andean System (Colombia and Venezuela), and Caricom. There are also three 'non-group' members: Cuba, the DR, and Panama. In the case of Cariforum, the functions are limited to co-ordinating negotiations with the EU. In the case of Caricom, the procedures to formalise the 1997 decision to admit Haiti have not yet been completed. Moreover, progress in completing the establishment of the Caricom Single Market and Economy has been agonisingly slow.

The difficulties in giving operational effect to new relationships are illustrated in the fate of a recent proposal to forge a strategic alliance between the Caribbean and Central America, with the DR acting as a bridge. This proposal emanated from the new Fernandez Administration in Santo Domingo in 1998. It envisaged: 1) a creation of a free trade area embracing both sub-regions; 2) functional co-operation in the promotion of investment and tourism and in the liberalisation of sea and air transport services; and 3) support of external negotiations over NAFTA parity, the FTAA, the EU-ACP relationship, and the coordination of WTO negotiations. Step 1, agreement on a DR-Central American Free Trade Area, was completed in April 1998. Step 2, agreement on a DR-Caricom FTA, was completed in outline form in June 1998 but a follow-up meeting on goods to be exempted was aborted due to the DR's opposition to Caricom's position on the matter. The proposal for a Caribbean-Central American Strategic Alliance was noted at the Cariforum-Cuba summit in August 1998 but no decision was taken.

BOX 6.3

Proposed Caribbean-Central American Strategic Alliance: Summary Objectives

1. Creation of free trade area embracing CARICOM, CACM, the Dominican Republic, and Panama
2. Increased competitiveness of business enterprises
3. Investment promotion (domestic and foreign)
4. Liberalisation of air and sea transport services
5. Tourism promotion
6. Co-ordination of policies and strategies *vis-à-vis*:
   - Nafta parity negotiations
   - FTAA negotiations
   - Cariforum-EU negotiations
   - WTO negotiations

Source: Based on text of the proposal published in *ACS Bulletin*, March 1998, Vol. 1 No. 7, reprinted in FES/ACE 1998

It is fair to say that there is no strong enthusiasm for the Alliance, or for a Caricom-Central American FTA, on either side. Both sub-regions were preoccupied with the more immediate demands on their attention: Caricom with the EU negotiations and the banana question; Central America with its relations with the US and Mexico and with post-hurricane Mitch recon- struction. In addition, as with external trade negotiations, the technical and political requirements of simultaneously servicing a wide range of regional initiatives is a strain on the limited resources of small states. The danger is that government policies will be entirely reactive to short-term pressures as they arise; with a consequent neglect of policies that are guided by long-term strategic planning.

Conclusions: Strategic Responses to Globalisation

Responding to globalisation evidently requires a 'walking on two legs' strategy. The one involves strengthening the bargaining position and nego- tiating capacity of the region's states in their external economic relations. The objective is to maximise the possibilities of outcomes that take account of the interests of small states with the specific production structures of the Caribbean. The other involves strengthening the productive and competitive capacities of regional producers to participate successfully in markets that will be increasingly hemispheric and global in scope. This requires techni- cally proficient strategic planning by governments, with industrial policies aimed at diversifying production, strengthening technological capabilities, and promoting innovation. The overall need is to increase the capacity of small economies to respond at the level of governments, firms and the population as a whole. With this in mind, the following suggestions are advanced.

The world financial crisis should be seen as a 'window of opportunity' for the South to insert itself into the redesign of the architecture of the international financial and monetary system. It will need to generate technically rigorous reform proposals that are in the interests of the South as a whole, while taking account of the heterogeneous nature of the countries comprising the South. The immediate dangers are those of 1) continuing instability resulting in a global economic depression that im- pacts further on the lives of hundreds of millions, and 2) negotiation of a new system among the US, the EU, and Japan that fails to take account of the interests of the South, with the latter becoming split into currency zones dominated by the US dollar, the Euro, and the Yen, respectively.

Together with the rest of the South, Caribbean countries should challenge the principles of universalistic neo-liberalism on which current international trade and economic negotiations are based, and seek recognition of the principles of selectivity, sequence, particularity, pluralism, and learning. Each state should have room to develop its own mix of industrial policy with regard to the role of the state, the private sector, and small-scale and community-based enterprises consistent with the objectives of equitable, participatory, and sustainable development.

As an integration grouping, Caricom needs to complete the establishment of the Single Market and Economy in order to strengthen its own bargaining power in regional and international negotiations.

In its external relations, Caricom needs to look beyond Lome and neo-colonial preferential arrangements, defining its strategic long-term interests in common with that of the smaller developing countries, beginning with the non-English-speaking Caribbean and Central America. One option is for Cariforum to be broadened into a co-operation mechanism, as a stepping stone to a Small Country Strategic Alliance between Caricom, the non-Caricom Caribbean (Cuba and the Dominican Republic), and Central America. The objective of a Small Country Strategic Alliance would be to lobby, bargain, and negotiate in favour of the principle of special and differential treatment in trade agreements for small countries and ministates, on the basis of their size-related environmental, economic, and social vulnerability.

Notes

1. The proposed REPAS were intended to embody EU/ACP Regional Trade Areas in which at least 80 per cent of all trade between the two partners would be liberalised, growing to 90 per cent within ten years of establishment to conform with WTO rules. The following provides a summary of the findings of studies carried out on the subject:
    1. The Caribbean (Caricom including Haiti, and the DR)
    With hemispheric trade liberalisation as under the proposed FTAA, the REPA would have 'very little trade creation and economic and revenue adjustment effects'. Absent an FTAA, the cost to CARICOM, and to a lesser extent the DR and Haiti, would be 'severe'. Tariff cuts from the REPA are unlikely to result in lower prices to Caricom consumers. Adjustment problems could be reduced if sensitive products were excluded from the REPA.

2. The Economic and Customs Union of Central Africa (CEMAC)

Impact on exports from Cemac to the EU would be zero, for Congo negligible, and for Gabon noticeable but slight. Only Cameroon would enjoy significant export gains. Cemac imports from the EU estimated to increase by 5 per cent. Most Cemac countries are customs revenue-dependent and would need to make changes to their fiscal systems to replace lost revenue. The overall impact of the REPA for Gabon, Cameroon, and Equatorial Guinea could be slightly positive; for the other lower income countries, lost customs revenues would be a problem. Cemac countries face technical and institutional constraints in redesigning their tax systems.

3. East African Economic Community (EAC)

EAC imports from the EU should increase as well as cause trade diversion by displacing more efficient non-EU suppliers. Potential customs revenue losses are substantial, especially for Kenya. Significant adverse effects on domestic producers are unlikely in Tanzania and Uganda, but probable in Kenya. Positive long-term effects are more likely due to increased investment in tradables.

4. The Pacific region

There is little experience of free trade in this region apart from that within the Melanesian Spearhead Group (MSG). There are problems due to lack of product complementarity and large differences in size, diversification, and competitiveness among them. Even an EU-MSG REPA would be problematic, 'as the MSG does not have a secretariat to handle complex trade negotiations'. The priority for Pacific ACP countries should not be 'to hurry into free trade arrangements with the EU'.

5. Southern African Development Community (SADC)

All the LDCs of the SADC- Angola Lesotho, Malawi, Mozambique, Tanzania and Zambia – 'would be better off without a REPA', due to customs revenue losses, greater competition both in domestic markets and in regional export markets. Non-LDCs could benefit, but a number of reasons make it difficult to establish a REPA in the SADC region, mainly because of a lack of integration within the SADC itself.

Studies commissioned by the EU show that the proposed Free Trade Areas would at best lead to marginal increases in ACP exports to the EU, with more significant increases in EU exports to ACP countries. Many ACP countries would face severe adjustment problems due to loss of customs revenue. Some ACP groups, notably the Pacific and Southern Africa, are also not yet ready for the internal free trade that is a requirement of the REPAs. It may be significant that the EU's proposals for REPAs were developed before the commissioning of studies on the likely impact. This suggests that they stemmed from prior commitment to free trade objectives rather than from an empirical analysis of the costs and benefits of the proposed arrangements to the ACP countries.

Source: Author's summary of Report in EUROSTEP (1998)

References

AP 1999, 'Global economy "inherently unstable" : Japan finance official', *The Ottawa Citizen*, March 20, 1999

Amin, Samir, *Capitalism in the Age of Globalisation* (London: Zed Books, 1997)

Chomsky, Noam, *Neoliberalism and Global Order: Doctrine and Reality*, 1998 (http://aidc.org.za/archives/chomsky)

Chossudovsky, Michel, *The Globalisation of Poverty: Impacts of IMF and World Bank Reforms* (Zed Books and Third World Network, 1997)

Clary, Isabelle, 'US Treasury Chief proposes global financial reforms', Reuters, October 1, 1998

Dasgupta, Biplap, *Structural Adjustment, Global Trade, and the New Political Economy of Development* (London: Zed Books, 1998)

Durbin, Andrea, 'Joint NGO Statement On The Multilateral Agreement On Investment [MAI]', revised: November 7, 1997 (e-mail: adurbin@essential.org)

Ekins, Paul and Manfred Max-Neef, eds., *Real-Life Economics: Understanding Wealth Creation* (London: Routledge, 1992)

Eurostep, 'Commission Free Trade Area Arrangement Studies Are Not Positive on FTAs with the ACP', November 20, 1998

Ferriol, Angela, 'La Reforma Economica en Cuba en los 90'/'Economic Reform in Cuba in the 1990s', *Pensamiento Propio*, No. 7, pp. 5–24, 1998

Fischer, Stanley, 'On the need for an International Lender of Last Resort', paper delivered at IEA, January 3, 1999 (see IMF website)

FTAA, Summit Of The Americas: Fourth Trade Ministerial Meeting, San Jose, Costa Rica. March 19th, 1998: Joint Declaration (visit http://www.ftaa-alca.org/EnglishVersion/costa_e.htm)

G24, Communique, April 26, 1999

Gill, Henry S., *The NAFTA Problematique and the Challenges for the Caribbean Community* (Miami, North-South Centre, 1991)

Girvan, Norman, 'Cuba: Structural Adjustment with a Human Face?', *Pensamiento Propio*, No. 7, pp. 25–30, 1998

Gonzales, Anthony, *The Impact of NAFTA on Caribbean Industry: Trade and Investment Effects.* Unpublished study prepared for UNIDO, October 21, 1995

Halimi, Serge, 'Liberal dogma shipwrecked', *The GuardianWeekly*, Vol. 159, No. 17; October 25, 1998

Hirst, Paul and Grahame Thompson *Globalisation in Question* (Cambridge: Polity Press, 1997)

Korten, David C., *When Corporations Rule the World* (London: Earthscan Publications, 1995)

Lewis, Patsy, 'Beyond Bananas: Globalisation; Size and Viability in the Windwards Islands', paper presented at Department of Government Seminar on Globalisation and Small States, UWI, January 13. 1999

Mander, Jerry and Edward Goldsmith, eds., *The Case Against The Global Economy and For A Turn To The Local* (San Francisco: Sierra Club, 1996)

McWhirter, Cameron and Mike Gallagher, 'Contributions buy influence', *The Cincinnati Enquirer*, Sunday May 3, 1998 (visit http://enquirer.com.contributions_buy.html)

Moseley, Paul, Jane Harrigan and John Toye, *Aid and Power: The World Bank and Policy-Based Lending* (London: Routledge, 1991)

Oxfam, 'A future for Caribbean bananas?', Oxfam briefing paper, London, February 1998

Phillips, Michael M., 'US Plans Punitive Tariffs in Dispute with EU', *The Wall Street Journal*, December 22, 1998, p. A2

Polanyi, Karl, *Primitive, Archaic and Modern Economies*, ed. George Dalton (New York: Anchor Books, 1968)

Report, *Overcoming Obstacles and Maximizing Opportunities: A Report by The Independent Group of Experts on Smaller Economies and Western Hemispheric Integration*, August 1997 (unpublished)

USIS, 'Bananas: US To Seek WTO Approval for Trade Sanctions, Jan. 25', *Washington File*, January 12, 1999

UNDP, *Human Development Report*, 1997

UNCTAD, 'UNCTAD advocates financial safeguard mechanism', TAD/INF/2759, August 25, 1998

7

Globalisation and Small Developing Countries
The Imperative for Repositioning

RICHARD BERNAL

Small, developing countries which are vulnerable to external events and that have limited adjustment capacity are particularly exposed to the effects of globalisation. The changes encompassed by globalisation have far-reaching implications for small developing countries. Indeed, the overall impact is one that makes change in small developing countries an imperative that must be addressed with urgency. These economies can reduce the adverse implications of globalisation and take advantage of the opportunities through a process of 'strategic global repositioning'.

Globalisation

Globalisation is a multi-dimensional process which is transforming at a rapid rate and in a profound way all aspects of national and global activities and interactions. The pace, extent and character of globalisation differ among the economic, political and social. It is a process in which barriers to the international flow of goods, services, capital, money, and information are being increasingly eroded and/or eliminated. This process is well advanced and in many respects, is irreversible.[1]

Global integration is evident in the accelerating growth of international trade and capital flows since World War Two. Trade grew in the first two decades after 1950, slowed perceptibly in the period 1974 to 1984, recovered between 1984 and 1989, and has grown rapidly since 1990. For the period 1950 to 1994, the volume of world trade grew at a rate of 1.6 times faster than that of world production, varying from a low of 1.2 during the 1970s to a high of 2.8 in the 1990s. During these years the value of world output increased by a factor of 5, while the value of world trade in goods multiplied by a factor of 14.[2] The WTO calculates that the ratio of world trade in goods and services to output increased from 15 to 22 per cent between 1974 and 1994 and estimates that it increased from 7 to 15 per cent over the period 1950 to 1974; i.e. it has more than tripled since 1950.[3] In recent years, international trade and capital flows have grown at a faster rate than world GDP. During 1983–93, there was a 71 per cent increase in the volume of world merchandise exports, double the 35 per cent growth in world output.[4] Since 1970 flows of direct foreign investment have grown at rates in excess of those at which international trade and world output have expanded. [5] During 1991–1996, direct foreign investment inflows increased by 24.4 per cent, far in excess of GDP and exports of goods and services that expanded by 10.7 per cent and 14.3 per cent respectively.[6]

Globalisation involves the creation of larger economic units through expansion, mergers and acquisitions by multinational corporations, and the coalescing of national economies through regional integration to form regional trade blocs.[7] Trade blocs have increased in importance both in terms of the share of world trade they encompass and the number of countries that participate in them. The number of regional trade agreements notified to the GATT/WTO has increased since 1948,[8] with a dramatic increase taking place during the last decade. By early 1999 there were 194 agreements of which 87 were established since 1990. Intra-regional trade has grown rapidly throughout the world since the late 1940s and now accounts for 59 per cent of world trade,[9] accounting for almost 70 per cent of trade in Western Europe.[10] The emergence of regional trade blocs, either market induced or politically engineered, represents a transition from an atomistic world economy of national economies to a global market. The proliferation of regional trade arrangements is simultaneously a response to globalisation and a factor shaping globalisation.[11]

Character of Globalisation

Globalisation is a multidimensional process that includes the following dimensions:

1. Economic

The economic dimension of globalisation includes the following features:

a) Dominance of the Global Market

Essentially, there is only one market – the world market. Management guru Peter F. Drucker explains that 'every business must become globally competitive, even if it manufactures and sells only within a local or regional market. The competition is not local anymore – in fact it knows no boundaries. Every company has to become transnational in the way it is run.'[12] Globalisation is not only integrating trade, investment and financial markets. It is integrating consumer markets and consumption patterns. Local and national tastes are yielding to global social standards and aspirations in consumption. 'Global elites' and 'global middle classes' follow the same consumption styles, showing preferences for 'global brands'. There are the 'global teens', some 270 million, 15–18 years old in 40 countries, inhabiting a 'global space', a single culturally homogenous world of the same videos, films, computer games, music and designer clothes.[13]

International media, particularly from the United States, disseminate a vast volume of films, television programmes, music, books, magazines, and computer software that is increasingly creating a global popular culture. Indeed, entertainment around the world is dominated by American-made products, which are purveyors of American values and views on politics, wealth, individuality, gender, violence, dress, sex and so on. United States distribution[14] is the largest in global terms. For example, Blockbuster Entertainment Corporation has 2,000 outlets in twenty-six countries, *Readers Digest* has 48 international editions in 19 languages; *Cosmopolitan* magazine has 36 foreign editions and *Playboy* magazine has 16 international editions.

b) Intensification of competition on a world scale

The implication of global competition is that even goods and services that are produced and exchanged within the national domestic sphere have to meet standards of quality and costs of production that are set globally. For example, in the early 1960s in the United States, the country with the largest domestic market, only 4 per cent of US domestic production was subject to international competition; today it is over 70 per cent.[15] The fusion of computer technology with telecommunications makes it possible for firms to relocate an ever-widening range of operations and functions to wherever cost-competitive labour, assets, and infrastructure are available. The new technologies make it feasible to standardise, routinise and coordinate activities that previously were subject to the friction of space and therefore regarded as non-tradable. They enable such activities to be turned into 'real-time' activities.

Competition has intensified not only among firms but also among countries, as all countries are increasingly exposed to the global market. Developing countries can no longer plan for the continued existence of preferential trading arrangements. The developed countries no longer feel obliged to provide preferential trade arrangements to developing countries[16] with minute markets, no indispensable raw materials, and limited strategic importance. Small developing countries in particular must be prepared to adapt to the elimination or erosion of preferential trade regimes, such as the LOMÉ Convention and the Caribbean Basin Initiative.

c) Growth of services

The average annual growth in trade in commercial services between 1980 and 1993 was 7.7 per cent, compared to 4.9 per cent for merchandise trade. The overall share of services in total trade amounted to 22.2 per cent in 1993 (up from 17 per cent in 1980), and it is estimated that in the early 1990's service industries accounted for 50 to 60 per cent of total foreign direct investment flows.[17] Furthermore, services account for 61 per cent of GDP in industrialised countries and between 35 and 51 per cent of GDP in developing countries.[18] The United States generates 72 per cent of its GDP in the form of services. Services accounted for 30 per cent of US exports[19] and jobs in the service sector accounted for 75 per cent of total employment.[20] In Great Britain and Switzerland, service industry exports, especially financial and tourism services, have already exceeded the export of goods.

d) Facilitating technology

The increasing globalisation of economic transactions and activities has been facilitated, and in some instances impelled by, rapid development of new technologies of communications, informatics, and manufacturing. New technologies have reduced transaction time, eliminated geography and distance, thereby creating an environment of 24-hour trading. In this environment the 'mindset must be speed'[21] The new developments in information processing and telecommunications propel globalisation by eliminating the costs resulting from distance, the importance of location and the advantages of large size. For example, the cost to transmit a 42-page document from New York to Tokyo by airmail would be US$7.40 over two days, by courier US$26.25 over 24 hours; by fax US$28.83 over 31 minutes and by e-mail $0.10 over two minutes.[22] The cost of a commercial bank transaction on the Internet is roughly one US cent, dramatically less than that of any other distribution channel, i.e. a cost of US$1.07 by the bank branch, US$0.73 by the mail; US$0.54 by telephone payment; US$0.27 by ATM; and US$0.01 by the Internet.[23] These technological developments have started to transform organisation structures, the nature of work, and the character of products, production techniques and international marketing. Indeed, the so called 'death of distance' will revolutionise the way people live and work[24] as we enter what has been called an 'age of globally networked intelligence.'[25]

e) Disembedded Finance

The global financial system underwent three revolutions almost simultaneously: deregulation, internationalisation, and innovation[26] and new technology (telecommunications and computers) which have transformed cross-border activity in financial services.[27] Financial flows have become disembedded from the real economy, with much of the global financial flows being unrelated to production, trade and investment. This has been compounded by the emergence of global financial markets with a dramatic shift 'from a financial structure which was predominantly state-based with some transnational links, to a predominantly global system in which some residual local differences in markets, institutions, and regulations persist as vestiges of a bygone era.'[28] The magnitude of the flows have dwarfed the resources of central banks and have reduced considerably the capacity of even the industrialised countries to control these flows.[29] Transactions in foreign exchange markets have now reached the astonishing sum of around $1.2 trillion a day – over fifty times the level of world trade. Around 95 per cent of these transactions are speculative. The daily volume of transactions on the foreign exchange market of the world total some $900 billion – equal to France's GDP – and some $200 million more than the total foreign currency reserves of the world's central banks.[30] The significant increase in short-term financial flows and reduced regulatory capacity of governments has caused a growing vulnerability to the disruptions that result from instability of short-term funds.[31] The instability in short-term funds has been a major factor in banking crises and exchange rate collapses in Mexico and the recent Asian crisis. Global financial markets also heighten the speed and extent of the spread of financial contagion.[32] While new mechanisms for crisis prediction, prevention, and management are urgently needed there is no consensus on proposals ranging from reform of the IMF[33] to new global institutions for financial surveillance and regulation.[34]

f) Electronic commerce

Electronic commerce (e-commerce) is a major development in the global economy. It involves business conducted on the Internet and other network based data inter-change systems. E-commerce will continue to affect fundamentally the way economic activities are conducted in financial services, telecommunications, entertainment, and various other services. Internet access and use is likely to grow rapidly. Estimates of Internet growth vary. US Government estimates indicate that in December 1995, approximately 10 million people were using the Internet, but 3 years later the number had jumped to 140 million.[35] Worldwide, from a base of 4.5 million users in 1991 and 60 million in 1996, the number was projected to rise to roughly 300 million by the end of the last century.[36] Electronic commerce is predicted to involve $300 billion by the end of the year 2000.[37] By 2003, Internet could account for 2 per cent of all commercial transaction.[38] It is estimated that in 1998 on-line commerce revenues amounted to $12 billion.[39]

2. Corporate Reorganisation

Multinational corporations (MNCs) now account for about a third of world output and two-thirds of world trade. A quarter of world trade is made up of intra-firm transactions taking place within multinational corporations.[40] They also account for half of world trade in manufactured goods and eighty per cent of the world's land cultivated for export crops.[41] Their prominence and 'global reach'[42] is such that Greider regards the MNC as being at the centre of what he calls 'the manic logic of global capitalism'.[43] In 1996, 85 of the top 100 MNCs were headquartered in the Triad, i.e. US, Europe, and Japan and their dominance is evident in ownership of foreign assets, foreign sales, and foreign employment.[44] Amoroso describes this phenomenon as 'the triadic capitalism of the transnational corporations'.[45] Concomitant with the dominance of MNCs in the Triad was the absence of firms from developing countries in the 1,000 largest companies in the world.[46]

Corporate reorganisation has taken a number of forms including down-sizing of administrative and managerial super-structures, strategic corpo-rate alliances[47] both through joint ventures and outsourcing, mergers, real-time activities, and global webs. [48] The most prominent feature of corporate reorganisation in recent years has been mergers and acquisitions, including cross-border mergers and acquisitions, which account for one quarter of all mergers and acquisitions worldwide and 58 per cent of direct foreign investment flows.[49] The total value of mergers and acquisitions in 1998 was $2.45 trillion, an increase of 54 per cent over 1997 and up by 613 per cent from $0.4 trillion in 1992.[50] While the number of mergers per annum has fluctuated over the last decade, nine of the ten largest mergers occurred during the past year, eight of them in the last six months. Mergers and acquisitions in emerging markets have increased in recent years.[51] Mergers impact on competition, consumer's interest, and barriers to entry, transcending national regulatory systems and tax avoidance – and on the continued emergence of a transnational-owning class.

3. Political

A global convergence of economic, technological, and ideological forces which drive the process of globalisation is shifting power away from governments toward multilateral institutions, and a small number of multi-national corporations and financial institutions [52] increasingly wield eco-nomic and political influence. Multinational corporations are estimated to account for a third of world output and two-thirds of world trade.[53] Con-comitant with the globalisation of economic processes, which is proceeding rapidly, there is a tendency for the nation-state to fragment, particularly where there are long-standing religious, racial, tribal, and ethnic differ-ences. Some have gone as far as proclaiming the demise of the nation-state,[54] certainly in an economic sense, but also increasingly as a viable political actor. This seems premature, as the nation-state has not been superseded by any political formation. However, sovereignty in all its dimensions has been constrained considerably[55] by economic interdependence. The weak-ening of allegiances to the nation-state [56] is understandable at the psycho-logical level because globalisation and its homogenising influence erode the basis for national allegiances, with the result that people are increasingly resorting to allegiances which are more tangible, easily discernible, and traditional. This tendency is made more pronounced by the bifurcation of national economies/societies between those who are active participants in, and beneficiaries of, the global economy and society, and those whose economic activities, cultural practices, and traditional lifestyles are threatened or, as importantly, perceived to be threatened, by globalisation.[57]

Globalisation will require increased international co-operation on worldwide issues, such as sustainable development. This will necessitate a trade-off between national sovereignty and multilateralism. National governments will not willingly relinquish management of national and international issues but governments will have less control over the design and implementation of national and international economic policy. Policies will have to be much more closely calibrated and flexible. For example, while it may be desirable to move towards free trade in goods and services, it may not be feasible to permit the completely unregulated flow of short-term money which has produced such instability in exchange rates. The rationale for free trade in goods cannot provide a justification for free capital mobility, as both history and recent events confirm the need for judiciously applied restraints on capital mobility. There is a reluctance to surrender national sovereignty, consequently attempts to expand rule-making on the multilateral level will face serious political limits.

The policy options available to the nation state are increasingly restricted and dictated by globalisation. The framework of policies, which enables a country to participate in international economic processes and to be viewed favourably by global corporations, has been described as the 'Golden Straitjacket'.[58] To compete successfully in global markets, countries have to remove obstacles and barriers to entrepreneurship, capital, and technology. Institutional change is advised because the policy imperatives

> . . . are unlikely to be met where the legal system fails to provide adequate protection to property rights and respect for the sanctity of contracts; where the political system cannot or will not provide stability and security; and where the social system does not encourage transparency and displays a high degree of tolerance for corruption and nepotism.[59] (Elliott Zupnick, 1999)

The role of the state has changed and will continue to change as the process of globalisation proceeds. Markets, both global and national, have reduced the dominance of government in economic affairs,[60] and together with changing political and economic thinking, will impact on the nature and the role of the state, perhaps leading to a 'third way'[61] which is neither state-control nor *laissez-faire*. There are many social services and economic goods which markets cannot be relied upon to provide [62] which raises the issue of the effectiveness of the state,[63] regardless of the role to be performed. Not only will government have to be 'reinvented' but also the very nature of the political process within the nation-state is likely to undergo profound change.[64]

4. Social

A prominent feature of globalisation is the widening gap between developed countries and the majority of developing countries. This is reflected in differences in income levels and other indicators of human well-being. The decline in the value of unskilled labour to production and labour-saving technological innovations have had a deleterious effect on employment in developing countries.

a) Widening rich-poor gap

The process of globalisation is highly uneven in the world economy, and although causality cannot be definitely established, is associated with an increasing gap between the rich and the poor. The concentration of private foreign investment among the OECD countries and the marginal-isation of sub-Saharan Africa are the most dramatic examples. Many of the bases of comparative advantage of the developing countries are no longer valid; for example cheap labour is of declining importance in manufacturing and even in agriculture. Technology has also reduced the importance of natural products and increased the efficiency with which primary products are utilised. The terms of trade for the least developed countries have declined a cumulative 50 per cent over the past 25 years. The share of the poorest 20 per cent of the world's population in global income is 1.1 per cent, down from 1.4 per cent in 1991 and 2.3 per cent in 1960. The ratio of the income of the top 20 per cent to that of the poorest 20 per cent rose from 30 to 1 in 1960 to 61 to 1 in 1991 – and was at 84 to 1 in 1995.[65]

Prospects are not good for closing the gap, particularly for the least developed countries. The World Bank's projection for growth in developing countries for the period 2002-08 is that it will be lower than in the 1990s.[66] In the last two years, *The Economist*'s index of industrial-commodity prices has fallen by 30 per cent. In real terms commodity prices are at their lowest since this index was first published a century and a half ago.[67] The disparities in growth are not likely to be reduced while 92 per cent of foreign direct investment is received by only 28 per cent of the world's population.[68] This is compounded by the fact that direct foreign investment in developing countries is highly concentrated. During the 1990s, nine of the 147 developing countries received 90 per cent of all direct investment flows.[69]

b) Labour

The deregulation of markets, the mobility of capital, and the foot-loose character of multinational corporations have forced workers in all countries to compete for jobs. Given that it is not only technologically possible and economically advantageous to manufacture goods in poor Asian, Latin American or African countries with unregulated labour markets, the bargaining power of workers in advanced countries has been eroded. Indeed, it has been argued that there has been a decisive shift in the balance of power between capital and labour to the disadvantage of workers.[70] Wage levels in developed countries, it is argued, are undermined by globalisation, the industrialisation of Asia and the products made by 'cheap' labour in developing countries.

It is widely believed in the United States and Western Europe that imports from developing countries are driving down wages and transferring jobs overseas.[71] Empirical evidence, however, has revealed that globalisation and developing-country imports have had only a modest effect on wages, employment, and wage and income inequality in the advanced economies.[72] The shifts in the types of employment, which appear to be associated with globalisation, emanate from new technologies such as robotisation and computerisation and corporate strategies, which put a disproportionate burden of adjustment on workers.[73] There has been a decline in low-skilled labour costs in total production costs in many global industries. The decline is estimated to be from an average of 25 per cent in the 1970s to between 5 and 10 per cent at present.[74] These developments have reduced job security[75] in all economic activities, prompting one commentator to speak of the 'Age of Insecurity.'[76]

5. Governance

The emergence of an increasingly globalised and integrated world economy raises the question of its management. The post-World War II economy was atomistic, consisting of national economies, and was managed by the Bretton Woods institutions (IMF and World Bank) and the GATT. This system reflected the existing polarisation of the Cold War and the hegemony of the United States. The delinking of the US dollar from gold in August

1971 marked the end of this institutional structure for global management. The end of the Cold War and the relative decline of US dominance has left an increasingly globalised and interdependent world economy without a hegemony to ensure decision-making and to enforce the rules.[77] In the 1960s the US-dominated international manufacturing trade contributed 25 per cent of all international trade flows, whereas in the 1990s its share of world manufacturing trade dropped to just 12 per cent.[78] This is best illustrated by the inability of the US to stabilise international currency markets as the international reserves of the G7 countries and the IMF are dwarfed by international currency flows. The decline of US hegemony[79] has caused a shift towards co-operation, which recognises the tripolar[80] economic configuration at present and requires a consensual decision-making process. A global architecture of rules must increasingly replace power-based international decision-making. However, a genuinely democratic and multilateral system of rules and management is not even in its embryonic stage.

The emergence of a global market has prompted some observers to call for the elimination of formal managerial institutions and to advocate that the global marketplace be untethered by national governments and international agencies.[81] In some situations, private-sector institutions could regulate their own activities.[82] A pure market approach, i.e. let the chips and the workers fall where they may, would be neither fair nor politically feasible. For example, in this scenario, the IMF would not assist countries in difficulties nor would governments assist in the structuring of private financial institutions. The fall-out from this type of global governance would be the diminution or elimination of institutions that would supervise and regulate the operation of global markets. The solution obviously lies somewhere between these two extremes, a dilemma reflected in the recent debate in the US over the role of the IMF and whether it should be given increased resources. The hands-off, free-market approach denigrated the IMF for bailing out profligate governments and bankrupt private banks. Indeed, it is claimed that the existence of the IMF has encouraged poor management by both the public and the private sector.[83] The opposing view regards the IMF as not sufficiently interventionist and advocates both more funding and earlier, preventative intervention. Yet another approach is to scale down the role of institutions like the IMF.[84]

One of the ironies of globalisation is that increasing interdependence and the creation of global markets would logically require increasing liberalisation. However, as liberalisation proceeds there has been a proliferation of rules and international dispute-settlement mechanisms. The Uruguay Round, which established the WTO, also substantially liberalised the mul-

tilateral trade regime in terms of reduced tariffs and quantitative restrictions and expanded coverage to include services, intellectual property
rights, and agricultural commodities. The irony is that trade liberalisation
has resulted in more disputes being referred to the WTO than at any time
previously. Since the inception of the WTO dispute-settlement mechanism
in January 1995, there have been over 150 disputes.[85] As national barriers
to international transactions are progressively reduced or eliminated, the
need to standardise national regimes becomes imperative. The adverse
implications of inadequate national regulatory regimes require multilateral
discipline. A multilateral rule-based regime, however, is only as strong as
its weakest link. Consequently, as globalisation proceeds, it will necessitate
better regulatory regimes and a standardisation of rules across countries.

6. Cultural

The rapid and profound technological changes which have occurred in
recent years have ushered in a new era in the world economy, which is
distinguished by a comprehensive globalisation of all spheres. Advances in
electronic data interchange, establishment of systems for the computer-
controlled trans-shipment and clearance of goods, improved voice and data
communication networks, automated banking, and international telemar-
keting have defined the nature of international relations. Global society and
international politics have been transformed by developments in telecommunications technology, which have revolutionised the speed and conduct
of all aspects of global interaction – economic, social and political. The
instant global availability of information via satellite, computers and telecommunications technology has the potential to change, irrevocably, all
aspects of human life.

A global mass culture has emerged as a result of economic globalisation,
international availability of media and international migration. Within this
overarching development there is simultaneously homogenisation, and
cultural complexity because cultures are not obliterated. Cultures are
nevertheless 'de-territorialised'[86] and cultural differences are increasingly
found within societies, and to a lesser extent between societies.[87]

It is culture which binds societies together and ensures that social
interaction is practiced on the basis of commonly accepted norms and
behaviour patterns. The accompanying homogenisation of ideas and behaviour patterns reduces cultural diversity. This is particularly evident in young
people, who are the most exposed to global media, the least immune, and

who consequently exhibit a remarkable similarity in taste and consumption patterns. Modern societies cannot be insulated against the media and further integration into a global society, but do not have to succumb to a homogenisation of global culture,[88] which is functionally integrated with global production and consumption.

In political relations, the integrity of the nation-state, the notions of sovereignty and national identity all require re-examination, given these global changes. Global media have aggravated tensions between developed and developing countries, as they reveal for all to see the vast gap in standards between rich and poor, exacerbating social contradiction and international tension. At the same time, global communications media have also established world public opinion as a potent force in international relations and a significant factor in the internal politics of countries, as evidenced in the liberation of South Africa and the implosion of communism.

Small developing countries have been continuously exposed to international media in the form of books, magazines, periodicals, radio broadcasts and, more recently, TV channels, particularly those originating in North America, transmitted by satellite technology. This has had a profound impact on lifestyles, consumer habits and patterns of behaviour. To the extent that exposure has escalated, there is corresponding dilution of national identities, as external influences permeate all aspects of life and begin to change, or at least threaten, the uniqueness of national identities.[89]

7. Psychological

Technological developments in telecommunications, computerisation, and informatics have eliminated the barriers of distance and time, resulting in the reconstitution of the world into a single social space.[90] The contemporary process of globalisation engenders an intensification of economic, financial, cultural and social cross-border interaction and growing awareness of this reality.[91] It is accompanied by processes of disintegration, as traditional political, social, and economic structures are eroded, and new ones are beginning to emerge. Globalisation at the cultural level is reflected in the emergence of 'global consciousness'. Global consciousness is manifested as a social matrix of people all over the world, unified through mass communication. Today, people have social relations and even organised community relations regardless of space, i.e. regardless of the territory that they share. This has enormous consequences not only for the role of the nation-state as a territorially bounded community, but also, for the organisation of economic production on a cross-border basis. It permits the emergence of 'imagined' communities, cultures, and even systems of authority and social control that traverse borders.

Globalisation increasingly creates a mindset of thinking globally and seeing the world as a single entity. Robertson describes this as 'the intensification of consciousness of the world as a whole'.[92] However, as it weakens the distinctiveness of national identities, an even more assertive defense of the differences in language, culture, myth, and fantasy is emerging. As it brings societies closer together, makes us all neighbours, and destroys the boundaries of identity and even national and regional consumption styles, the reaction is to cling to sub-national differences that remain. At the same time that economic forces and the availability of information have become global, there has been a countervailing movement towards smaller social units. This is evident in a major resurgence in nationalism and ethnicity. Even as the nation-state yields to the amalgamation of the national economies into transnational blocs, there is an accompanying psychological impact, characterised by a feeling of being overwhelmed and disoriented. Individuals seek, but often can no longer find, a secure sense of identity in the political and social formation of the nation-state. Inevitably, identity begins to be located in culture, race, language and ethnicity, which both transcend and fragment the society and the nation-state. The individual's attachment to smaller groups can threaten traditional national identity.

Small Developing Countries

The number of countries and states in the world has increased significantly in recent decades; in particular, there has been a proliferation of small states and economies. At the end of World War One, there were 62 independent countries, by 1946 that number had risen to 74 and currently stands at 193. Most of these are small states. Indeed, 87 countries have a population of less than 5 million, 58 have under 2.5 million people, and 35 have less than 500,000 people.[93] The majority of these small states are developing economies.

Small states, especially small developing economies, can be significant beneficiaries of globalisation or can be overwhelmed by the challenges of competing with larger, more developed countries. Small developing economies are very open economies, and it is claimed that they will benefit more from free trade than any other type of economy. These countries, it is suggested, should liberalise as comprehensively and as rapidly as possible. According to an OECD study, 'countries that have been more open have achieved double the annual average growth of others . . . enjoy higher rates of private investment.'[94]

Over the period 1985–95, the developing countries that achieved the fastest economic growth were the countries that, as a group, had the highest ratios of imports and exports to GDP. Medium and low-growth countries had import and export ratios that were roughly half as large as the fast-growing countries.[95]

Specifically, the countries which have achieved the highest rates of economic growth, mainly the newly industrialised countries of Asia, are supposed to have achieved this by free-trade policies. The fundamental weakness in this argument is the assumption that all economies are alike and therefore have similar capacities to adjust and seize the opportunities of free trade. This paradigm does not adequately take account of size of economies. Small developing economies are a sub-set of the genre of small economies. These economies differ from other economies in structural characteristics, which have implications for the character of the growth process and the capacity for adjustment.

1. Vulnerability

Vulnerability in small developing countries is derived from the structure of these economies, which reflect their small size.

a) A high degree of openness

External transactions are large in relation to total economic activity, as indicated by the high ratio of trade to GDP. There is heavy reliance on external trade because of a narrow range of resources and the inability to support certain types of production, given the small scale of the market. Economic openness is measured by imports and exports of goods and services as a percentage of GDP.

b) Export concentration

The limited range of economic activity in small economies is reflected in concentration on a limited number of exports accompanied, in the majority of cases, by a relatively high reliance on primary commodities. In extreme cases, one primary product export accounts for nearly all of exports; for example, in 1991 bananas accounted for 92 per cent of total exports in Dominica and 87 per cent in St Lucia; phosphate was 91 per cent of exports in Nauru; and timber amounted to 69 per cent of exports in the Solomon Islands.[96] Export concentration is compounded by the dependence on one or two export markets, for example, Britain absorbs 80 per cent of Dominica's bananas and 90 per cent of St Lucia's exports.

There is a high degree of openness, that is, the trade/GDP ratio is high. The high degree of openness and the concentration in a few export products, particularly primary commodities whose prices are subject to fluctuations in world markets, make small economies vulnerable to external economic events and expose them to real shocks of an intensity unparalleled in larger countries.[97] Economic vulnerability can be a feature of an economy of any size and level of development, but it is compounded by a small size, a tendency to natural disasters, remoteness, and insularity. Studies of developing countries have demonstrated that there is a direct relationship between vulnerability and size, with the smallest developing countries being the most vulnerable. The World Bank/Commonwealth Secretariat study shows that of 111 developing countries, 26 of the 28 most vulnerable were small countries and the 28 least vulnerable were all large states.[98] Canada, Brazil, Argentina, and the United States have vulnerability indexes of 0.2 or less, while Caribbean and Central American economies exceed 0.4. The ten smallest economies range from 0.595 for Barbados to 0.843 for Antigua.[99]

2. Volatility

Volatility is a pronounced characteristic of developing countries, which export a few primary products, particularly minerals and agricultural commodities,[100] and experience erratic fluctuations in capital. Volatility in small developing countries also entails susceptibility to natural disasters and a severely constrained adjustment capacity. Volatility is costly since it reduces economic growth because of its adverse impact on investment, resource allocation, productivity, financial intermediation, inflation, exchange rates, and income distribution.[101] Small states experience higher income volatility than larger states. As estimated by the World Bank/Commonwealth Secretariat, 'the standard deviation of annual real per capita growth is about 25 per cent higher'.[102]

a) Export instability

Small economies have traditionally experienced export instability because
of their dependence on a few primary product exports. Many small economies have tried to reduce export instability by shifting to services, particularly tourism and financial services. However, the change in export composition toward the service industry has been accompanied in some cases by
higher instability in export earnings.[103]

b) Volatility of capital flows

Capital flows in developing countries exhibit significant volatility, as in
Latin America's case.[104] A recent study of FDI flows in the last 20 years
reveals that small developing countries are at a disadvantage in attaining
FDI relative to larger developing countries. Even when they have sound
economic policies, small developing countries are rated 28 per cent more
risky.[105]

c) Susceptibility to natural disasters

One of the peculiarities of small developing countries, particularly small
islands, is the prevalence of natural disasters.[106] The impact of a natural
disaster on a small economy and its financial sector can be far more
devastating than it is on a large economy, where the damage is relatively
localised. For example, the damage to Jamaica from Hurricane Gilbert in
1988 amounted to about 33 per cent of GDP; to Antigua from Luis and
Marilyn in 1995, to about 66 per cent of GDP; to Montserrat from Hugo in
1989, to about 500 per cent of GDP. In comparison, the damage to the United
States from Hurricane Andrew in 1992, while much larger in an absolute
amount, amounted to only 0.2 per cent of GDP.[107]

d) Constrained adjustment capacity

Volatility is pronounced in small developing economies because of structural rigidities and institutional weakness resulting in limited adjustment
capacity. Their adjustment process is more difficult, larger relative to GDP,
and of necessity slower than the adjustment process for larger economies.[108]
One feature, which has restricted fiscal policy and trade liberalisation, is
the high dependence on trade taxes as a percentage of government revenue.
Trade taxes account for more than one-half of government revenue in St

Lucia, Belize, and the Bahamas, and over one-third of government revenue in Guatemala and the Dominican Republic.

3. Lack of International Competitiveness

Small economies have severe constraints on their material and labour inputs both in amount and variety, because of their limited land area and small populations. These constraints make it very difficult to attain global standards of efficiency and economies of scale for a wide range of products and lead to high unit costs of production. Small economies tend to have a narrower range of domestic and export production because of the small size of the market and the limited range of resources. Small market size also tends to cause high costs because there is often a lack of competition. In fact, in many instances the market can only support a single product – creating a monopoly. Concentration is usually significantly higher in developing countries than in developed countries, for example in manufacturing.[109] This is particularly true in the case of small developing countries where small domestic markets make it difficult for firms to attain economies of scale and, if they do, it is usually by market dominance, in many instances as monopolies.[110]

Firms in small economies, especially small developing economies, are all small by comparison with firms in large or developed countries and multi-national corporations. The total sales of the largest US firm, General Motors, is 328 times larger than the biggest Caribbean firm, Neal and Massey of Trinidad and Tobago. Wal-Mart, the largest employer in the United States, has a staff complement of 675,000 compared to the Caribbean's top employer, Lascelles Demercado of Jamaica, which employs 6,800.[111] Export firms in small developing countries are minute by global standards, for example 74 per cent of exporting firms in Jamaica have less than 100 employees.[112] Small firms even in developed countries are at a disadvantage compared to large firms. Small firms can attain neither internal economies of scale (where unit cost is influenced by the size of firm) nor external economies of scale (where unit cost depends on the size of the industry, but not necessarily on the size of any one firm). Small economies, and thereby small industries (including export sectors) are unlikely to foster the competitive dynamic necessary for firms in small economies to achieve competitive advantage.[113] Competitive advantage is more likely to occur when the economy is large enough to sustain 'clusters' of industries connected through vertical and horizontal relationships. Small firms in small developing countries have severe difficulties in attaining 'economies of scope', i.e. economies obtained by a firm using its existing resources, skills and technologies to create new products and/or services for export. Exposure to global competition requires small firms to invest heavily just to survive in their national market, and more so in order to export. Larger firms are better able to generate new products and sources from existing organisations and networks.[114]

Production is also burdened by higher costs for imports because small economies pay higher transportation costs.[115] Higher costs derive from the relatively small volume of cargo, small cargo units, and the need for bulk breaking. Small economies pay an average of ten per cent of the value of merchandise exports as freight costs, compared to a 4.5 per cent worldwide average and an 8.3 per cent developing countries' average.[116] The private sector has to bear the cost of sub-optimal public sector operations, and this increases their cost of production.

The public sector in small economies accounts for a larger share of GDP, which reflects a certain indivisibility of public administration structures and functions – every country, no matter how small, has a prime minister, a parliament, a police force, etc. The growth of the public sector has been due in part to an enhanced role for public sector investment in the economy which, however, has been associated with reduced growth.[117]

Imperatives For Change

The world economy is not changing; it has already changed. The only thing that is certain is change itself, and change at an exponential rate. The ability to discern changes, to adopt and adapt new technology and rapidly reorganise will ultimately determine the capacity to respond. Firms, governments and individuals must get accustomed to the lack of permanence and not resist change but recognise that it is unavoidable and represents both challenge and opportunity. The countries which succeed in the new globalisation are the countries, which pursue 'pro-active adjustment', that is, they adjust quickly, in anticipation of, and in response to global changes in demand and technology. Those countries which pursue 'reactive adjustment', that is, react to events late and defensively by focusing on protectionism, are not going to survive, and will not achieve growth. It is not possible in this new globalisation to insulate production or demand from global competition and changes. Therefore, it is not possible for small developing economies to achieve growth if they opt for the route of protectionism.

There must be pro-active adjustment, which improves competitiveness in the global market place.

Small developing economies are a particular genre of economy and therefore have particular characteristics, which affect their capacity to achieve sustained economic development.[118]Given the profound changes which are taking place in the global economy and the speed of these changes, small developing economies must adapt to this new environment. Successful adaptation can best be achieved by a process of strategic global repositioning.[119] This process involves the formulation and implementation of a strategic plan of repositioning a country in the global economy. Such plans are designed to consolidate and improve existing production lines while reorienting the economy toward new types of economic activities for both the national and global markets. In most developing countries, this involves structural transformation, not merely adjustment, to achieve economic diversification, in particular export diversification.

Strategic Global Repositioning

Strategic global repositioning is a process of repositioning a country in the global economy by implementing a strategic plan. Such a plan is designed to consolidate and improve existing production while reorienting the economy by creating new types of economic activities. In most small developing countries, this means structural transformation, not structural adjustment, to achieve economic diversification, in particular export diversification. The need for strategic global repositioning is derived from trends in the global economy, and the composition of exports of small, developing economies, which is skewed toward primary products. Strategic global repositioning must be accompanied by policies which improve the competitiveness and efficiency of companies, by creating a stimulating entrepreneurial environment. Selective trade, fiscal and credit policies supported by medium-term education, technology policies focused on 'strategic sectors', and close co-operation between government and the business sector contribute to the targeted development of internationally competitive industries. Market-oriented and strategic state management, combined with the co-operation of companies, government agencies, research institutions, and funding institutions can create dynamic competitive advantages. These kinds of policies must be directed to long-term strategies to mobilise market forces, build up world-market-standard firms, and systematically develop efficient economic locations.

1. Envisioning New Development Perspectives

Small developing countries have traditionally attempted a transition from agriculturally based economies, which export primary products to an industrialised economy exporting manufactured goods. The motivations were obvious, given that industrialisation was regarded as synonymous with development and high per capita incomes. The conventional wisdom in development economics since the early 1950s has viewed industrialisation as a strategy for transforming developing economies into developed economies. All developing countries attempted industrialisation, in the vast majority of cases, by an initial phase of import-substitution industrialisation. Having nurtured infant industries by protectionist measures and incentives to foreign investment, economies were to become exporters of manufactured goods, capitalising on wage differentials between developed and developing countries, as well as taking advantage of raw material availability and energy, where available. However, very few developing countries succeeded in achieving this scenario. A few have become known as the newly industrialised economies, the most notable examples being the 'Asian Tigers'. Changes in the world economy which no longer require low-wage manufacturing and the very success of the newly industrialised countries have filled this niche in the international division of labour and the attendant industrialisation and export opportunities.

The option of industrialisation based on low wages is therefore no longer feasible for the majority of small developing countries. However, this is not the disaster that it appears to be, because, for some countries with the necessary attributes, it is both possible and desirable to relinquish the unquestioning faith in the procreative power of industrialisation, and to diversify to become service-oriented economies. The export of services can provide growth because services are the fastest growing component of the world economy. Like industrialisation, this is not an option, which every small developing country can pursue.

There must be both recognition of the need to change and a willingness to innovate. Every process of adjustment begins with a change of mind-set, outlook and attitude. This process of adjustment will only commence in earnest when there is a change of mind-set in both the public and private sector and entrepreneurs dare to think in new and adventurous terms. There has to be a paradigm shift, which should now be possible since reality so clearly contradicts the viability of the entrenched, dominant 'industrialisation paradigm'. The 'industrialisation paradigm' based on import stabilisation industrialisation behind protectionist barriers rationalised by 'infant industry' arguments has exhausted the national market. Regional integration proffered the solution of the amalgamation of economies into a regional market, which would permit economies of scale and improve efficiency through competition.[120]

2. Maintaining a Predictable Macroeconomic Framework

It is essential that stability in macroeconomic policy be sustained in the medium term in order to provide an environment conducive to investment and a minimum of disruption. The macroeconomic policy instruments such as fiscal policy, monetary policy, and exchange-rate policy must be applied in a consistent manner and complemented by an institutional framework which facilitates private sector-led, market-driven growth. Rodrik's study of developing economies concludes that 'the ability to maintain macroeconomic stability in the face of often turbulent external conditions is the single most important factor accounting for the diversity of post-1975 economic performance in the developing world.'[121] Domestic economic policies have a key role in reducing vulnerability to external contagion. A recent IMF study of foreign exchange market crises in the 1990s found that those worse affected exhibit pre-crisis inadequacy in economic fundamentals and institutional weaknesses.[122] Economic growth is most likely where macroeconomic policy measures are carefully calibrated with the microeconomic conditions necessary for structural adjustment[123] and supported by effective governance, the rule of law, entrenched property rights, and low barriers to international trade.[124]

Mobilising capital, technology, and the human skills necessary for effective competition in the global marketplace can be garnered in the global economy, provided that the national economic environment is attractive and stable. In addition to appropriate macroeconomic policies, the critical components of the national economic environment are a predictable institutional framework, consistent with current global standards and practices, for example, well-established property rights and strategic planning based on continuous dialogue and interaction between the leadership of the private sector, the public sector, the trade unions, and social sectors. This can be augmented by inputs from individuals and organisations abroad.

Close and continuous co-operation between the leadership of these sectors is essential in order to effectively formulate strategic planning and targeted implementation. What is needed is a marriage, which harnesses the vision and expertise of all sectors. This co-operation has been a critical factor in the economic success of Japan and the newly industrialised countries of Asia, particularly in promoting private-/public-sector synergy and the allocation of decisions between the market and public administration.[125]

3. Producing Competitive Exports

The outlook for the demand and prices of raw materials and primary products is not encouraging. Given the history of fluctuating commodity prices and declining terms of trade against manufactured goods, it is important that the products, which are exported, are competitive in price and viable in the medium to long term.

a) Export diversification

There has to be a willingness to look beyond traditional economic activities to the new dynamic sectors in the global economy, such as microelectronics, biotechnology, telecommunications, robotics, and information. A transition from economies dominated by low-wage and labour-intensive activities to technology-based and information-intensive activities is required. A glimpse of the opportunities can be gleaned from the fastest growing firms in the US, which are concentrated in computers (retailing, networking, software, manufacturing, health care, leisure/recreation and financial services).[126] Services are the fastest growing sector in world trade and the jobs created are relatively high-wage and environmentally safe. There are good prospects for the export of services to developed countries.

The need to focus attention on the expansion of new exports for the global market should not diminish attention to be given to other sectors and products. While the opportunities for growth in traditional sectors, such as agriculture and labour-intensive manufacturing, are not as propitious, these sectors should not be abandoned. Indeed, there may be complementarities and linkages. Complementarity between new and old sectors is clearly evident between tourism and agriculture in the small economies of the Caribbean.[127] What is required is balanced development emphasising diversification of exports by creating new exports while improving the competitiveness of traditional exports where feasible. Consolidating existing production by improving cost efficiency, enhancing and maintaining the quality of mineral processing, agro-industrial and manufacturing exports remain an important objective. The prevalence of outdated technology, low capacity utilisation, lack of inter-industry linkages and the shortage of skilled labour must be addressed. Expanding existing services such as tourism and informatics, which have attained international standards in productivity and are competitive in the global market place, is also important. Undoubtedly, there will be some new manufacturing industries in which small developing economies can successfully participate. In small developing countries the needed increase in productivity in traditional export industries and new economic activities can benefit from new technologies in both sectors. The widespread diffusion and application of information technology not only creates an industry in itself but also raises productivity in agriculture, manufacturing, and services. Services account for an increasing proportion of the value of all products. The expansion of a service sector is therefore not an alternative to traditional production but is complementary and a necessary component of all products.[128] The workforce will have to be more skilled, knowledge-oriented and capable of adapting to new technology. Management, production, and decision-making will have to be 'informationalised'.[129] Export firms will have to develop the capacity to respond quickly to changes in demand in existing and new markets in the world economy. This, more than anything else, is the secret of success of the newly industrialised export economies of Asia.

The travel and tourism industry is the largest industry in the world and the leading employer. It is also one of the fastest-growing sectors of the world economy, accounting for ten per cent of the world's employment and GDP.[130] Tourist arrivals are forecasted to grow by 4.3 per cent per annum over the next 20 years and receipts from international tourism by 6.7 per cent per year.[131] Tourism is already important in many small economies, such as those in the Caribbean where, in 1994, the tourism sector accounted for 24.5 per cent of the GDP; 18.7 per cent of employment; and 60 per cent of earnings from the export of goods and services in Barbados,[132] as was also the case in the Maldives.[133] However, if tourism is to continue to grow, it must diversify to include new products such as heritage tourism,[134] health tourism[135] and eco-tourism.[136]

The services sector in the US will provide 50–90 per cent of all new jobs in the United States between now and 2005.[137] Many of these millions of jobs, for example in informatics and accounting, can be undertaken in small developing countries given wage differentials and the availability of communications technology. With its relatively less expensive expertise, India is becoming a leader in informatics and the export of computer software. Today, software exports amount to US$1.75 billion, compared to US$500 million in 1993, and US$74 million in 1985.[138] The industry has continued to grow rapidly with 61 per cent of exports going to the United States[139] and almost 160 of the Fortune 500 companies out-source their software requirements to India.[140] Many small, developing economies have the right factor mix, lower wages, and close proximity to a major industrial country to be the site for back-office operations such as data processing, accounting and other business services. Swiss Air has moved its accounting department from Switzerland to Bombay, India[141] and Cigna, a large US healthcare company, is one of several US companies that have set up back offices in Ireland.[142] In the area of offshore financial services, the Bahamas and the Cayman Islands have been involved in offshore banking since the late 1970s.

The entertainment industry is one of the fastest-growing sectors of the world economy. The worldwide sales of recorded music have grown by more than 300 per cent, from US$12 billion in 1981 to US$39.7 billion by 1995.[143] Music from small developing countries, for example reggae music from Jamaica, has the potential to earn significant amounts of foreign exchange. Reggae recordings, sold in the United States, earned revenue of over $270 million and account for 14 per cent of the albums sold in the British market. Approximately 7 per cent of the albums sold in the UK are recorded or written by Jamaicans.[144] Film-making has significant potential, as a series of recent productions have demonstrated, but much more needs to be done to encourage this lucrative industry through, for example, an aggressive campaign to attract film companies and productions as is being done in Ireland.[145]

The high cost of health-care in the developed countries makes it cheaper for individuals to travel to small developing countries for treatment, for example, the northern Caribbean and Central America. An increasing number of Americans have been going to Mexico for treatment because the cost of a doctor's visit is as much as 80 per cent lower than in the US cost and some drugs are up to 75 per cent less expensive.[146] There is a growing trend towards persons in developed countries retiring abroad, particularly to developing countries with warm climate because their income purchases more abroad than in the USA. The market for retirement facilities will increase sharply in the next twenty years.[147] The small developing countries in close proximity to the developed countries, with year-round warm weather, and relatively lower wage levels, constitute an environment suitable for the development of retirement communities. Over the next 50 years, the global population over 65 years old will increase by 1 billion, nearly 50 per cent of total global population growth.[148] A decisive shift in the demographic structure of developed countries has already occurred. Approximately 9.2 per cent of the population in these countries was over 65 years old in 1960, increasing to 13.3 per cent in 1990 and is projected to reach 20.2 per cent in the year 2020.[149]

b) Revitalising Traditional Exports

Traditional sectors like export agriculture can be revitalised by improving the quality and price competitiveness of export staples, like sugar, bananas, and coffee. In addition, new export products should be explored. The export opportunities of the traditional sector have not been exhausted, but require some imagination and innovation, for example, exotic horticulture, banana chips, and 'tropical boutique agriculture'.[150] Recent successful non-traditional agro-exports to the USA include winter vegetables, high-value fruit and cut flowers.[151] New niche industries are emerging daily, such as export of butterfly pupae from Costa Rica.[152] Revitalisation requires a combination of increased productivity, product innovation, and the penetration or creation of niche markets. In recent years, Israel has been unable to compete in the European market with imports of citrus from Brazil, Morocco, and other developing countries. Israel's market has since developed new hybrids of citrus which are sweet, colourful, seedless, and easy to peel. Not only did exports of 'easy peelers' increase by 65 per cent over the last year, but Israel is also exporting the technology to non-competing countries such as South Africa.[153]

Manufacturing is a difficult option for small developing economies and tends to be viable when there are favourable circumstances, for example, the availability of raw materials or cheap energy as in the case of Trinidad and Tobago or special market access to industrialised countries, e.g. the apparel industries in Jamaica and the Dominican Republic which export under the auspices of the Caribbean Basin Initiative. The establishment of export processing zones has enabled some small, developing countries to maintain some manufacturing.[154] Computer technology and what Krugman[155] calls the 'slicing-up of the value chain' to produce goods in a number of stages in different locations, adding a little value at each stage, have reduced the importance of large-size producing units.

Defensive and reactive adjustment, which seeks the preservation of industries or the retention of aspects of production which can be accomplished at a lower cost in other countries, is self-defeating. In the short run, it reduces competitiveness of exports and provides higher priced goods to the national market, reducing demand and increasing inflation. In the long run, entrepreneurs will find ways to import cheaper alternatives and will relocate uneconomic aspects of production in other countries in order to retain international price competitiveness and national market share. In addition to innovation, productivity and competitiveness are increasingly determined by the generation of new knowledge or by access to, and processing of information. Small developing economies must seek to create a technologically advanced, information-based society, and keep up with customisation and informationalisation proceeding in such key sectors as the apparel industry.[156]

4. Improving Productivity

Globalisation necessitates continual improvements in productivity. In particular, attention will have to be given to increasing labour productivity, improving managerial capacity, and upgrading infrastructure.

a) Management

Management will have to become more sophisticated, keep abreast of developments in international markets, and constantly update itself on new technological innovations. Managerial capacity has improved considerably and professionalism has increased in recent years. However, there is still room for improvement, particularly in the public sector. In the short run the private sector's managerial capacity can be upgraded by importing skilled managers and other professionals. This need not mean that foreigners, unaware of the country's culture and traditions, should take over top managerial posts. In the short run there are more than enough skilled Caribbean professionals overseas who, under the right circumstances, would be willing to return home. Countries must no longer be viewed as physical places but as a 'nations without borders'. In the long run, this requires a re-orientation of post-secondary education away from an emphasis on the arts, and towards management, accounting, computer programming, and all aspects of modern technology.

In a business environment, characterised by frequent changes requiring rapid responses, management and workers must evolve a new relationship in which traditional roles and attitudes must be replaced by a collaborative interaction. The relationship between management and workers and between different levels within the production process will have to change in a way which ensures incentives and maximises productivity. The interaction within the workplace will have to be more co-operative and the divisions less rigid, permitting more dialogue between trade unions and management. If productivity is to be increased and innovations encouraged, it is imperative that the atmosphere becomes less adversarial and more genuinely interactive. The traditional notion of the worker will have to be abandoned and replaced by a new concept which recognises worker participation in managerial decisions and employee stock-ownership programmes. These developments will require trade unions to expand their traditional role beyond wages and working conditions to include employment creation/preservation, education/training, and ownership participation. The fact that the number of work stoppages and strikes has decreased in recent years is an indication that this process has already begun.

b) Labour

The productivity of labour of both workers and managers would need to be upgraded. This means improvement in the quantity and quality of education. The importance of this issue is illustrated by the experience of the East Asian countries. The expansion and transformation of education and training during the last three decades has been a key factor in the 'economic miracle' achieved by East Asian economies.[157] This has to be tackled both within the individual enterprise and in the society as a whole. Firms need to put more emphasis on vocational training and on-the-job education. The new technology of learning can make an important contribution in this regard. Multimedia training enables workers to learn faster and in more detail, particularly those workers who are functionally illiterate. For example, low-income countries cannot compete effectively when there are 1.6 personal computers per one thousand people in these countries compared to 199.3 per thousand in high-income countries.[158]

Increasingly, the world economy will be dominated by knowledge-based industries, especially services, making the quality of human capital a critical factor. In the case of many developing countries, much of their human capital resides outside their borders. Every effort must be made to repatriate such capital. Just as incentives and special programmes exist for foreign investment, similar schemes must be established to encourage overseas nationals with professional skills to return home. It might even be necessary to run an advertising campaign to attract skilled foreign professionals as is now being done aggressively by the Government of Canada.[159] Overseas communities and returning professionals and businessmen have spear-headed several of the new growth sectors in India, such as computer hardware and software.[160]

c) Infrastructure

There is an urgent need to improve the extent and quality of physical infrastructure such as roads, irrigation, electricity, and telecommunications in order to reduce the operating costs of firms in all sectors. Road transpor-tation and telecommunications now require a quantitative leap in anticipa-tion of increased demand and must utilise state-of-the-art technology. Under the right conditions, much of the required expansion in physical infrastructure could be financed by private capital, including foreign capi-tal. This has already begun to happen in electricity generation and airport expansion. The improvement in infrastructure must focus not only on modernisation but must take cognisance of the need to close the gap with developed countries. For example, developing countries cannot compete effectively where telephone main lines per 1,000 inhabitants are 25.7 in low-income countries, compared with 546.1 in high-income countries.[161]

5. Modernise International Marketing

There are problems with production in small developing countries, such as inconsistent quality, irregularities in supply, and poor labeling. Inadequate marketing has also been a severe constraint on exports. There are some sectors which have achieved sophisticated levels of marketing in some services, notably tourism. In some instances these weaknesses have been obviated by strategic corporate alliances, commodity agreements, and sub-contracting. However, much can be done to catch up with new market-ing techniques and technologies,[162] and with interactive electronic market-ing in particular.[163] Interactive retailing, which is growing rapidly in devel-oped countries,[164] can take many forms, including personal computer-users linked to on-line services and Internet-based retailers, multimedia kiosks, interactive home shopping programmes over cable and satellite TV net-works, and CD-ROM-based shopping catalogues. All of these formats allow the consumer to purchase by telephone or computer and pay by credit card, while allowing the retailer reduced costs of storage and display areas for products.[165] The necessity to develop electronic marketing is suggested by the fact that in the US, which is the largest single market, more than one-third of all households own personal computers and the number is growing at approximately 35 per cent per year.[166] The number of Internet subscribers has grown from 25 million in 1993 to 90 million in 1995 and was projected to be 1 billion by the year 2000.[167]

6. Forging Strategic Corporate Alliances

Corporate integration, consolidation, and restructuring through cross-border mergers and acquisitions is a worldwide phenomenon. This has resulted from striving for size, and reorganisation, consolidation, and pruning in preparation for more intensive competition in the global market place.[168] Another response to competition has been the formation of strategic business alliances. These arrangements have superseded bitter political differences and economic rivalry. As a result China and Taiwan are involved in petro-chemicals,[169] Toshiba (Japan) and Samsung (Korea) collaborate on chips,[170] Air France and Lufthansa on hotel chains, Meridian and Kempinski share marketing and reservation systems[171] and Nissan buys auto parts from a Toyota affiliate.[172]

Some firms and financial institutions from small developing countries have become multinational corporations. However, the vast majority are very small. A merger movement among nationally-owned firms would make these firms more viable and more attractive joint-venture partners with foreign investors. This is critically important in the export sectors because most exporters are small compared to the multinational corporations against which they have to compete in the world market and major export markets such as the United States and Europe. Small size puts exporting firms at a severe disadvantage and, therefore, there is a need for corporate alliances[173] or mergers which can provide access to capital, expertise, management and technology.[174]

Concluding remarks

Differences in size between states and economic units, particularly those whose operations are global, are an important dimension of globalisation, which has not been given sufficient attention. This issue needs to be addressed urgently both by individual small, developing countries and by the global community as a whole. Small developing countries need to commence immediately a process of strategic global repositioning. At the international level, disparities in size must be addressed by ensuring that the international regulatory regime and institutions incorporate sensitivity to this problem. In the same way that national governments make provisions for small farms and small businesses, the global community must mediate the encounter between small countries and small economic units and their larger counterparts in the global marketplace. In this regard, nearly all economic units operating in, or from, small developing countries are small by global standards.

Notes

1. Roger Burbach and William I. Robinson, 'The Fin De Siècle Debate: Globalisation as Epochal Shift', *Science and Society*, Vol. 63, No. 1 (Spring 1999), pp. 10–39; Gray, John, *False Dawn: The Delusions of Global Capitalism* (London: Granta, 1998), p. 206; A. Glyn and B. Sutcliffe, 'Global but leaderless? The new capitalist order', in Miliband, R. and L. Panitch, eds., *The New World Order: The Socialist Register* (London: Merlin Press, 1992) pp. 76–95; Hirst, Paul and Grahame Thompson, *Globalisation in Question* (London: Polity Press, 1996); and Paul Sweezy, 'More or Less on Globalisation', *Monthly Review*, Vol. 49, No. 4 (1997), p. 1–4

2. *International Trade: Trends and Statistics*, 1995 (Geneva: World Trade Organisation, 1995) p. 15

3. Ibid, p. 17

4. Preeg, Ernest H., *Trade Policy Ahead: Three Tracks and One Question* (Washington, DC : Centre for Strategic and International Studies, 1995), p. 6–7

5. *Liberalising International Transactions in Services: A Handbook* (New York and Geneva: United Nations, 1994), p. 14

6. World Investment Report 1997, *Transnational Corporation, Market Structure and Competition Policy* (Geneva: United Nations, 1997), p. 4

7. Bernal, Richard L., *Trade Blocs: A Regionally Specific Phenomenon, or Global Trend?*, Walter Sterling Surrey Memorial Series (Washington, DC : National Planning Association, September, 1997)

8. *Regionalism and the World Trading System* (Geneva: World Trade Organisation, 1995) p. 25

9. *Trade Blocs and Beyond: Political Dreams and Practical Decisions* (Washington, DC : World Bank Draft Policy Research Paper, December 6, 1999) p. 1–6

10. Hege Northeim, Karl-Michael Finger, and Kym Anderson, 'Trends in the Regionalisation of World Trade, 1928 to 1990', in Anderson, Kym and Richard Backhurst, eds., *Regional Integration and the Global Trading System* (New York: St Martin's Press, 1993) pp. 436–486; and World Trade Organisation, Annual Report 1996, Vol. II (Geneva: World Trade Organisation, 1996) p. 23

11. Oman, Charles, *Globalisation and Regionalisation: The Challenge for Developing Countries* (Paris: Organisation for Economic Co-operation and Development, 1994); and Hettne, Bjorn, Andras Inotai and Osvaldo Sunkel, eds., *Globalism and the New Regionalism* (London, Macmillan Press, 1999)

12. Peter F. Drucker, 'Beyond the Information Revolution', *The Atlantic Monthly*, October 1999, p. 51

13. Human Development Report, 1998 (New York: Oxford University Press for the United Nations Development Program, 1998)

14. Paul Farhi and Megan Rosenfeld, 'American Pop Penetrates Worldwide', *Washington Post*, October 25, 1998

15. Steven Cohen, 'Geo-economics and America's Mistakes' in Carnoy, Martin, ed., *The New Global Economy in the Information Age* (London: McMillian, 1993) p. 98

16. Bernal, Richard L., *Sleepless in Seattle: The WTO Ministerial Meeting of November 1999* (forthcoming)

17. World Bank, *Global Economic Prospects and the Developing Countries*, 1995 edition (Washington, DC : World Bank, 1995) p. 47-48

18. *Liberalising International Transactions in Services: A Handbook* (New York and Washington DC : United Nations Conference on Trade and Development Programme on Transnational Corporations and the World Bank, 1993) p. 6-7

19. McRae, Hamish, *The World in 2020. Power, Culture and Prosperity: A Vision of the Future* (London: HarperCollins, 1994) p. 27

20. World Bank, *Global Economic Prospects and the Developing Countries*, 1995 edition (Washington, DC : World Bank, 1995) p. 48

21. Davis, Stan and Christopher Meyer Blur, *The Speed of Change in the Connected Economy* (New York: Time Warner Books, 1999)

22. Martin, Chuck, *Net Future: The 7 Cybertrends That will Drive Your Business, Create New Wealth, and Define Your Future* (New York: McGraw Hill, 1999), p. 15

23. Martin, Chuck, op.cit., p. 30

24. Cairncross, Frances, *The Death of Distance: How the Communications Revolution Will Change Our Lives* (Boston: Harvard Business School Press, 1997)

25. Tapscott, Don, *The Digital Economy: Promise and Peril in the Age of Networked Intelligence* (New York: McGraw-Hill, 1996)

26. Solomon, Robert, *Money on the Move* (Princeton University Press, 1999) p. 109

27. Herring, Richard J. and Robert E. Litan, *Financial Regulation in the Global Economy* (Washington, DC: Brookings Institution, 1995) p. 13

28. Stopford, J. and Susan Strange, *Rival States, Rival Firms* (Cambridge University Press, 1991) p. 40–41

29. Millman, Gregory J., *The Vandal's Crown: How Rebel Currency Leaders Overthrew the World's Central Banks* (New York: The Free Press, 1995)

30. Gray, John, *False Dawn, The Delusions of Global Capitalism* (London: Granta, 1998) p. 62.

31. French-Davis, Ricardo and Stephany Griffith-Jones, *Coping with Capital Surges: The Return of Finance to Latin America* (Boulder: Lynne Rienner, 1995)

32. Goldstein, Morris, *The Asian Financial Crisis: Causes, Cures and Systemic Implications* (Washington, DC: Institute for International Economics, 1998), p. 17–22

33. Eichengreen, Barry, *Toward a New International Financial Architecture: A Practical Post-Asia Agenda* (Washington, DC: Institute of International Economics, 1999)

34. Eatwell, John and Lance Taylor, *Global Finance at Risk: The Case for International Regulation* (New York: The New Press, 2000)

35. 'Net Commerce', *Financial Times*, December 3, 1998

36. *Electronic Commerce and the Role of the WTO* (Geneva: World Trade Organisation, 1998), p. 10

37. *Electronic Commerce and the Role of the WTO*, op.cit., p. 1

38. *Electronic Commerce and the Role of the WTO*, op.cit., p. 10

39. Furey, Tim R., 'Why Profits Still Elude E-Commerce', *The Journal of Commerce*, January 21, 1999

40. UNCTAD, World Investment Report, 1994 (Geneva: UNCTAD, 1994)

41. Stopford, John and Susan Strange, *Rival States, Rival Firms* (Cambridge University Press, 1991), p. 15

42. Barnet, Richard J. and Ronald E. Mueller, *Global Reach: The Power of the Multinational Corporation* (New York: Simon and Schuster, 1974)

43. Greider, William, *One World, Ready or Not: The Manic Logic of Global Capitalism* (New York: Simon and Schuster, 1997), pp. 20–26 and 55–223

44. United Nations, World Investment Report, 1998 Trends and Determinants (Geneva: United Nations, 1998), p. 39

45. Bruno Amoroso, *On Globalisation: Capitalism in the 21st Century* (New York: St Martin's Press, 1998) p. 2

46. ' The Business Week Global 1000, Country by Country', *Business Week*, July 13, 1998, pp. 59–77

47. Gomes-Casseres, Benjamin, *The Alliance Revolution: The New Shape of Business Rivalry* (Cambridge: Harvard University Press, 1996)

48. Hoogvelt, Ankie, *Globalisation and the Post-colonial World* (Baltimore: Johns Hopkins University Press, 1997) pp. 125–128

49. United Nations, World Investment Report, op.cit., p. 19

50. Sherer, Paul, M., 'The Lesson From Chrysler, Citicorp and Mobil: No Companies Nowadays Are Too Big to Merge', *The Wall Street Journal*, January 4, 1999

51. Frances Williams, 'Mergers may lift foreign direct investment to more than 800 billion', *Financial Times*, September 28, 1999

52. Strange, Susan, *The Retreat of the State: The Diffusion of Power in the World Economy* (Cambridge University Press, 1996); and Korten, David C., *When Corporations Rule the World* (Hartford: Kumarian Press and San Francisco: Barrett-Kochler, 1995)

53. Gray, John, op.cit., p. 62.

54. Ohmae, Kenichi, *The End of the Nation-State* (New York: Free Press, 1995); and Reich, Robert B., *The Work of Nations* (New York: Alfred A. Knopff, 1991)
55. Wriston, Walter B., *The Twilight of Sovereignty* (New York: Charles Scribner's Sons, 1992); Hirst, Paul, and Grahame Thompson, *Globalisation in Question* (New York: Polity Press, 1996), ch. 8; and Sassen, Saskia, *Losing Control? Sovereignty in an Age of Globalisation* (New York: Columbia University Press, 1996)
56. Buchanan argues that globalism is causing allegiance to shift from nation-state to ethnocentrism. Buchanan, Patrick J., *The Great Betrayal: How American Sovereignty and Social Justice are Being Sacrificed to the Gods of the Global Economy* (New York: Little, Brown, 1998)
57. Moss Kanter, Rosabeth, *World Class: Thriving Locally in the Global Economy* (New York: Touchstone, 1995)
58. Friedman, Thomas L., *The Lexus and the Olive Tree* (New York: Farrar, Strauss, Giroux, 1999) pp. 83-92
59. Zupnick, Elliott, *Visions and Revisions: The United States in the Global Economy* (Boulder: Westview, 1999) p. 4
60. Yerkin, Daniel and Joseph Stanislaw, *The Commanding Heights: The Battle Between Government and the Marketplace that is Remaking the Modern World* (New York: Simon & Schuster, 1998)
61. Giddens, Anthony, *The Third Way: The Renewal of Social Democracy* (Cambridge: Polity Press, 1998)
62. Kuttner, Robert, *Everything for Sale: The Virtues and Limits of Markets* (New York: Twentieth Century Fund, Alfred, A. Knopf, 1997); Hutton, Will, *The State We're In* (London: Jonathan Cape, 1995)
63. *The State in a Changing World*, World Development Report 1997 (Washington, DC: World Bank 1997)
64. Guehenno, Jean-Marie, *The End of the Nation-State* (Minneapolis: University of Minnesota Press, 1995); Davidson, James Dale, and William Rees-Moss, *The Sovereign Individual* (New York: Simon and Schuster, 1997)
65. United Nations Development Programme, *Human Development Report*, 1997 (Oxford University Press, 1997)
66. Global Economic Prospects and the Developing Countries 2000 (Washington, DC: World Bank, December 1999) p. xi
67. 'Could it happen again?', *The Economist*, February 20, 1999, p. 19
68. Hirst, P., and G. Thompson, *Globalisation in Question* (London: Polity Press, 1996), p. 68
69. World Bank, *Global Economic Prospects and the Developing Countries* (Oxford University Press, 1997)
70. Wolman, William and Anne Colamosca, *The Judas Economy: The Living of Capital and the Betrayal of Work* (Reading, Massachusetts: Addison-Wesley, 1996)
71. Aaron Berstein, 'Backlash Behind the Anxiety Over Globalisation', *Business Week*, April 24, 2000, pp. 52–53; and Goldsmith, Sir James, *The Trap* (New York: Carrel & Graf, 1994) p. 20

72. Burtless, Gary, Robert Lawrence, Robert Litan and Robert J. Shapiro, *Globaphobia: Confronting Fears about Open Trade* (Washington, DC: Brookings Institution, 1998); Matthew Slaughter and Philip Swagel, 'Does Globalisation Lower Wages and Export Jobs?' (Washington, DC : International Monetary Fund, *Economic Issues*, No. 11, 1997); Martin Wolf, 'Trade is not to Blame', *Financial Times*, December 10th, 1996

73. Gordon, David M., *Fat and Mean: The Corporate Squeeze of Working Americans and the Myth of Managerial Downsizing* (New York: Free Press, 1996)

74. Oman, Charles, *Globalisation and Regionalism: The Challenge for Developing Countries* (Paris: Organisation for Economic Co-operation and Development, 1993) p. 17

75. Stennett, Richard, *The Corrosion of Character: The Personal Consequences of Work in the New Capitalism* (New York: WW Norton, 1998)

76. Elliot, Larry and Dan Atkinson, *The Age of Insecurity* (London: Verso, 1998)

77. On the role of a hegemony in managing the world economy, see Kindleberger, Charles P., *The World in Depression, 1929-39* (Berkeley: University of California Press, 1973); Block, Fred L., *The Origins of the International Economic Disorder* (Berkeley: University of California Press, 1977); and Cohen, Benjamin J., *Organising the World's Money* (New York: Basic Books, 1977)

78. Ankie Hoogvelt, p. 123

79. There is a debate over whether US hegemony has declined and whether this decline is absolute or relative. See Kennedy, Paul, *The Rise and Fall of Great Powers* (New York: Vintage Books, 1987); Nau, Henry R., *The Myth of America's Decline* (Oxford University Press, 1990); Nye, Joseph S., *Bound to Lead: The Changing Nature of American Power* (New York: Basic Books, 1990); and White, Donald W., *The American Century: The Rise and Decline of the United States as a World Power* (New Haven: Yale University Press, 1996)

80. Thurow, Lester, *Head to Head: The Coming Economic Battle Among Japan, Europe and America* (New York: William Morrow Co., 1992), pp. 203-218; Ohmae, Kenichi, *Triad Power: The Coming Shape of Global Competition* (New York: Free Press, 1985); Thurow, Lester C., *The Future of Capitalism* (New York: William Morrow and Co., 1996), ch. 7

81. Milton Friedman, 'Markets to the Rescue', *Wall Street Journal*, October 13, 1998

82. Charles Calomiris, 'The IMF's Imprudent Role as Lender of Last Resort', *CATO Journal*, Vol. 17, No. 3 (Winter, 1998)

83. James K. Glassman, 'The World Doesn't Need a Financial Big Fix', American Enterprise Institute for Public Policy, *On the Issues*, October 1998

84. Henry Kissinger, 'Perils of Globalisation', *Washington Post*, October 5, 1998

85. Elif Kaban, 'WTO caseload rise linked to credibility', *Journal of Commerce*, November 5, 1998

86. King, Anthony D., ed., *Culture, Globalisation and the World System* (Minneapolis: University of Minnesota Press, 1997) p. 6

87. Hannerz, Ulf, 'Scenarios for Peripheral Cultures', in King, op.cit, pp. 107–128

88. Richard Barnett and John Cavanagh, 'Homogenisation of Global Culture', in Mander, Jerry and Edward Goldsmith, eds., *The Case Against the Global Economy* (San Francisco: Sierra Club Books, 1996), pp. 71–77

89. Dunn, Hopeton S., ed., *Globalisation, Communications and Cultural Identity* (Kingston: Ian Randle Publishing Limited, 1995)

90. Hoogvelt, Ankie, *Globalisation and the Post-colonial World: The New Political Economy of Development* (Baltimore: Johns Hopkins University Press, 1997) p. xiv

91. Waters, Malcolm, *Globalisation* (London: Routledge, 1995) p. 3

92. Robertson, Ronald, *Globalisation* (London: Sage, 1992) p. 8

93. 'Small but Perfectly Formed', *The Economist*, January 3, 1998, p. 65

94. *Open Markets Matter. The Benefits of Trade and Investment Liberalisation* (Paris: Organisation for Economic Co-operation and Development, 1998) p. 10

95. *World Economic Outlook* (Washington DC: International Monetary Fund, May 1996), p. 85

96. *Small States: Meeting Challenges in the Global Economy*, Interim Report of the Commonwealth Secretariat/World Bank Joint Task Force on Small States, October 1999, p. 15

97. Vincente Galbis, 'Mini-state Economies', *Finance and Development*, June 1984, p. 37

98. *Small States: Meeting Challenges in the Global Economy*, Interim Report of the Commonwealth Secretariat/World Bank Joint Task Force, October 1999

99. Lino Briguglio, 'Small Island Developing States and Their Economic Vulnerabilities', *World Development*, Vol. 23, No. 9 (1995) pp. 1615–32

100. *Overcoming Volatility: Economic and Social Progress in Latin America, 1995 Report* (Washington, DC: Inter-American Development Bank, 1995) p. 194

101. Op. cit., pp. 195–206

102. *Small states, Meeting Challenges in the Global Economy*, Interim Report of the Commonwealth Secretariat/World Bank Joint Task Force on Small States, October 1999, p. 13

103. Ransford Palmer, 'Export Earnings, Instability and Economic Growth, 1957 to 1986', in McKae, David L., ed., *External Linkages in Small Economies* (Westport: Praeger, 1994), pp. 31–34

104. Op. cit., pp. 194-195

105. Collier, Paul and David Dollar, *Aid, Risk and the Special Concerns of Small States*, Development Research Group, World Bank, February 1999

106. *A Future for Small States: Overcoming Vulnerability* (London: Commonwealth Secretariat, 1997), pp. 65–78; and Pantin, Dennis, *The Economics of Sustainable Development in Small Caribbean Islands*, (Mona, Jamaica: Centre for Environment and Development, University of the West Indies, 1994) p. 16

107. World Bank Report

108. Helleiner, G. K., 'Why Small Countries Worry: Neglected Issues in Current Analyses of the Benefits and Costs for Small Countries of Integrating with Large Ones', *World Economy*, Vol. 19, No. 6, (November 1996) pp. 759–63

109. Rodrick, Dani, 'Imperfect Competition, Scale Economies and Trade Policy in Developing Countries', in Balwin, R. E., ed., *Trade Policy Issues and Empirical Analysis* (Chicago: University of Chicago and National Bureau of Economic Research, 1988) pp. 109–137

110. Ali Ayub, Mahmood, *Made in Jamaica: The Development of the Manufacturing Sector* (Washington, DC: World Bank, Staff Occasional Paper, No. 31, 1981)

111. Richard Bernal, 'The Integration of Small Economies in the Free Trade Area of the Americas', CSIS, Policy Paper on the Americas, Vol. IX, Study No. 1 (Washington, DC: Center for Strategic and International Studies, February 2, 1998)

112. Harris, Donald J., *Jamaica's Export Economy: Towards a Strategy of Export-led Growth*, Critical Issues in Caribbean Development, No. 5 (Kingston: Ian Randle Publishers, 1997), table B. 01

113. Porter, Michael E., *The Competitive Advantage of Nations* (New York: Free Press, 1990), pp. 71–73

114. Knox, Paul, and John Agnew, *The Geography of the World Economy* (London: Edward Arnold, 2nd edition, 1994) pp. 95 and 218

115. Lino Briguglio, 'Small Island Developing States and their Economic Vulnerabilities', World Development, Vol. 2–3, No. 9 (1995) pp. 1615–1632

116. *A Future of Small States: Overcoming Vulnerability* (London: Commonwealth Secretariat, 1997) p. 29

117. Robert E. Looney, 'Profiles of Small, Lesser Developed Economies', *Canadian Journal of Development Studies*, Vol. 10. No. 1, (1989) pp. 21–37

118. Richard L. Bernal, 'The Integration of Small Economies in the Free Trade of the Americas', Policy Papers on the Americas, Vol. IX, Study I (CSIS, February 2, 1998)

119. Richard L. Bernal, 'Strategic Global Repositioning and the Future Economic Development of Jamaica', The North-South Agenda Papers, No.18, (Miami: North-South Center, University of Miami, May 1996)

120. Brewster, Havelock and Clive Y. Thomas, *The Dynamics of West Indian Economic Integration* (Kingston: I.S.E.R./University of the West Indies, 1967)

121. Rodrik, Dani, *The New Global Economy and Developing Countries: Making Openness Work* (Washington, DC: Overseas Development Council, 1999) p. 17

122. *World Economic Outlook, April 1999* (Washington DC: International Monetary Fund, 1999)

123. Winston Dookeran, 'Preferential Trade Agreements in the Caribbean: Issues and Approaches' in *Trade Liberalisation in the Western Hemisphere* (Washington, DC: Inter-American Development Bank and the Economic Commission for Latin America and the Caribbean, 1995) p. 467

124. Barro, Robert, *Determinants of Economic Growth: A Cross-country Empirical Study* (Cambridge: MIT Press, 1997)

125. Wade, Robert, *Governing the Market: Economic Theory and the Role of Government in East Asian Industrialisation* (Princeton: Princeton University Press, 1990)

126. Warren Cohen and John Simmons, 'Fast Companies', US News and World Report, Vol. 119, No. 1 (July 3, 1995), pp. 42–45

127. Janet Henshall Momsen, 'Caribbean Tourism and Agriculture', in Klak, Thomas, ed., *Globalisation and Neo-liberalism: The Caribbean Context* (Lanham: Rowman and Littlefield, 1998), pp. 115–134

128. Auliana Poon, 'New Implementation Challenges – A Flexible Specialisation Paradigm', *Nordic Journal of Latin American and Caribbean Studies*, Vol. 28, Nos. 1–2 (1998) pp. 71–72

129. Information technology has not merely added a new dimension to the way business is conducted, but has altered fundamentally the nature, management, and organisation of business. See Davis, Stan and Bill Davidson, *2020 Vision* (New York: Simon and Schuster, 1991)

130. Caribbean Group for Cooperation in Economic Development, *A Study to Assess the Economic Impact of Tourism on Selected Caribbean Countries* (The World Bank, May 1996)

131. Francesco Frangialli, ' Preserving Paradise,' Our Planet, Vol. 10, No. 1 (1999) p. 19

132. Op. cit., pp. 5 and 108

133. *Pacific Island Economies: Toward Higher Growth in the 1990s* (Washington, DC: World Bank, 1991) p. 62

134. Boniface, Priscilla and Peter J. Fowler, *Heritage and Tourism in the Global Village* (London and New York: Routledge, 1993)

135. George Alleyne, 'Health and Tourism in the Caribbean', Bulletin of PAHO, Vol. 20, No. 3, 1990, pp. 291–300

136. Doreen Hemlock, 'Costa Rica is planning eco-tourism theme park', *Sun-Sentinel*, December 10, 1996

137. *Occupational Outlook Handbook, 1992–93* (Washington DC: US Department of Labour, May 1992), p. 10; and Mazarr, Michael J., *Global Trends 2005* (New York: St Martin's Press, 1999) p. 121

138. Edward A. Gargan, 'India Among Leaders in Software for Computers', *New York Times*, December 29, 1993; N. Visuki Rao, 'India Posts 20% Growth in Software Exports', *Journal of Commerce*, February 28, 1994; and Paul Taylor, 'New IT Mantra Attracts a host of devotees', *The Financial Times*, December 2, 1998

139. Paul Taylor, 'Global Competitor with turnover of $1 billion a year', *Financial Times*, December 6, 1995

140. Paul Taylor, 'Remarkable Growth Rate Continues', *The Financial Times*, December 2, 1998

141. Daniel Green, 'SIA considers moving department to India', *Financial Times*, October 13, 1992

142. John Murray-Brown, 'Fiber Optic Bridge', *The Financial Times*, November 11, 1994

143. Ralph Henry and Keith Nurse, *The Entertainment Sector of Trinidad and Tobago: Implementing an Export Strategy*, (Port of Spain: Industry & Trade Division, TIDCO, October 1996) p. 5

144. Pamela B. Watson, 'The Situational Analysis of the Entertainment Recorded Music Industry', (Miami: Watson & Company Consulting Services, Inc., 1995)

145. Mike Burns, 'Michael D's Isle of Imagination , *Europe*, July/August, 1995, pp.18–19; and Hugh Linehan, 'Ireland makes its own luck', *The European Magazine*, August 3–9, 1995, p. 6

146. Phillip J. Hilts, 'Quality and Law Cost of Medical Care Lure Americans on Border to Mexico', *New York Times*, November 23, 1992

147. "The Economics of Aging', *Business Week*, September 12, 1994, pp. 60–68

148. Peterson, Peter G., *Grey Dawn: How the Coming Age Wave will Transform America and the World* (New York: Times Books, 1999) p. 31

149. Peterson, Peter G., op. cit., p. 13

150. Reyes-Pacheco, A., *An Option for Caribbean Agriculture Development: Tropical Boutique Agriculture*, (Kingston: Inter-American Institute for Cooperation on Agriculture, May, 1992)

151. Thrupp, Lori Ann, *Bitter Sweet Harvests for Global Supermarkets: Challenges in Latin America's Agricultural Export Boom* (Washington DC: World Resource Institute, August, 1995) pp. 18–19

152. Julie Dulude, 'Butterflies Aren't Free', *Latin Trade*, March 2000, p. 32

153. Mark Dennis, ' Israel pins expansion hopes on "television fruit"', *Financial Times*, July 6, 1995, p. 23

154. *Mauritius: Expanding Horizons* (Washington, DC: World Bank, 1992)

155. Paul Krugman, 'Growing World Trade: Causes and Consequences', Brookings Papers on Economic Activity, No. 1 (1995) pp. 333–335

156. John Waiter, 'Tomorrow is Here', *Bobbin*, Vol. 36., No. 11 (July, 1995) p. 39

157. *The East Asian Miracle* (Washington DC: World Bank, Oxford University Press, 1993), pp. 43-46

158. World Development Report 1998/99 (Washington, DC: World Bank 1998), p. 63

159. Lila Sarick, 'Canada strives to woo upscale immigrants', *The Globe and Mail*, June 7, 1995

160. Joyce Barnathan, et al, 'Passage Back to India', *Business Week*, July 17, 1995, pp. 44–46

161. World Development Report 1998/99 (Washington, DC: World Bank 1998), p. 63

162. 'Reinventing the Store', *Business Week*, November 27, 1995, pp. 84–96

163. Nicolas Denton, 'Advertisers eyeball the Net', *Financial Times*, March 17, 1997

164. Frederick Studemann, 'Germany's home shopping revolution starts to hot up', *Financial Times*, 18th November 1996

165. Tom Foremski, 'Interactive retailing: Latest technologies', *Financial Times*, October 4, 1995. See also 'Merchants of cyberspace', *Sunday Times*, November 19, 1995

166. Paul Taylor, 'Retailers wake up to "cyberspace"', *The Financial Times*, October 4, 1995

167. John Wiater, 'Tomorrow is Here', *Bobbin*, Vol. 36, No. 11 (July, 1995), p. 39
168. 'Feeding Frenzy on the Continent', *Business Week*, May 18, 1992, pp. 64–65
169. 'China Joins Taiwan-Led Chemical Deal in Malaysia', *The Journal of Commerce*, May 19, 1993
170. 'Toshiba to Work with Samsung on Flash Chips', *New York Times*, December 22, 1992
171. 'Feeding Frenzy on the Continent', *Business Week*, May 18, 1992, pp. 64–65
172. 'Nissan to Buy Auto Parts From a Toyota Affiliate', *The Wall Street Journal*, May 14, 1993
173. Badaraco Jnr., Joseph L., *The Knowledge Link: How Firms Compete through Strategic Alliances* (Boston: Harvard Business School Press, 1991); and Starr, Martin K., *Global Corporate Alliances and the Competitive Edge* (New York: Quorum Books, 1991)
174. Agmon, Tamir and Richard L. Drobnick, eds., *Small Firms in Global Competition* (New York: Oxford University Press, 1994)

8

Globalisation and Regional Economic Integration

BYRON BLAKE

The two often contradictory and overlapping trends of globalisation and regionalisation have dominated international economic relations in the last decade of the twentieth century. Simultaneously, the trends are mutually reinforcing and facilitating, on the one hand, and challenging and a source of reaction on the other. There is a school of thought which sees globalisation and the creation of regional blocs as diametrically opposite and competing concepts. One will eventually come to dominate. It is a recognition of this tension and an implicit acceptance of the likelihood of dominance of the globalisation trend which has prompted, I suspect from a regionalist perspective, the question which I have been asked to address: 'Globalisation and Regional Economic Integration'.

In addressing the issue, as posed, it should not escape us that the 'internationalists' perceive the threat very differently. They see the 'inexorable' movement towards the creation of mega regional economic blocs as a challenge to the global system. They see a fortification of exclusive blocs as creating zones of economic and potentially military conflicts.

We will look at the main features of globalisation as well as developments in regional integration and then draw some conclusions and implications for developing countries, more particularly for regional economic integration among developing countries.

Globalisation

Globalisation received a new dynamic beginning in the late 1980s after the strong challenge by third world countries to the increasing dominance of TNCs in the 1970s and the constraining impact of the Cold War in the 1960s and 1970s. The new thrust towards globalisation is being driven by technology, in particular communication technology; finance, in particular speculative capital; and corporate or production organisation.

Put differently, globalisation is being pushed by the corporate or business sector with governments creating the legal and institutional arrangements to support the phenomenon. The main legal and institutional arrangements include:

- The WTO, which has significant powers to enforce compliance by contracting parties to replace the GATT arrangements, which depended to a large extent on moral suasion and the will of contracting parties to co-operate
- Agreement to liberalise the trade in goods by:
    i) Establishing an upper limit on tariffs and a programme for reduction. Each contracting party has submitted a schedule of its existing tariffs on goods which have been negotiated, verified and bound
    ii) Determination to discontinue the use of non-tariff measures (NTMs) and to translate these into tariffs (tariffication) with a schedule for their reduction. NTMs include quantitative import restrictions, variable import levies, discriminatory import licensing, minimum import prices, and voluntary export restraints (VERs)
    iii) An agreement to bring agriculture within the ambit of the international agreement through specific commitments on market access, that is, the binding of tariffs and restraint in the use of non-tariff measures; domestic support; export competition; and even an agreement on the application of sanitary and phytosanitary measures. Developing countries have the flexibility to implement their reduction commitments over a period of up to ten years
    iv) An agreement on bringing trade in services within the multilateral framework of the WTO, to a progressive liberalisation of access to service providers and the application of national treatment
    v) An agreement bringing intellectual property rights within the WTO and the acceptance of strengthened rules to protect the trade in intellectual property. Intellectual property covers copyright and related rights, patents, trademarks, geographical indications, industrial designs, layout designs of integrated circuits and undisclosed infor-

mation. Patents are available for new inventions – products or processes – in the field of technology and the burden of proof of non-violation of the patent holder's right is now on the defendant

vi) The conclusion of a Protocol on Financial Services in the WTO

The institutional architecture for a globalised system of production, trade and finance is, however, not yet complete. Stimulated, in particular, by the financial crises in Asia and Russia and the contagion effects in Brazil, Argentina, and other Latin American countries such as Mexico and Venezuela, and a desire to use the psychological effect of a new millennium, there is increasing pressure to:

- Restructure the arrangements (the Bretton Woods Institutions) for managing global money and finance (the main proposals for this effort by President Clinton of the USA and Prime Minister Blair of the UK envisage this overhaul being undertaken by the dominant economic powers – the G-7)
- Inaugurate a 'millennium' round of trade negotiations which would focus significantly on agriculture, financial services, competition policy, environment, and labour standards as well as procurement.

In a number of areas, globalisation is also leading to overlapping jurisdiction among international organisations, conventions, and treaties. This includes:

- International Civil Aviation, where the drive to 'open skies', to introduce new technologies – including guidance systems – and to enhance safety and security is leading to tensions between the WTO and the International Civil Aviation Organisation (ICAO)
- International maritime transportation
- International telecommunications
- Various conventions and protocols on the environment.

Regional Economic Integration

Regional economic integration has been an important feature of international economic relations in the post-World War Two era. In spite of a lack of universal support, Customs Unions (CU) and Free Trade Areas were specifically permitted under GATT 1947. The relevant agreements or provisions are:

- Article XXIV of GATT 1947, which exempts state parties from the most-favoured nation (MFN) principle in establishing CUs and Free Trade Areas and sets the conditions for CUs and Free Trade Areas. A major requirement was that the Agreement must cover 'substantially-all-trade among the parties to the CU or Free Trade Area';

- Part IV on 'Trade and Development' – which was added to GATT in 1965 to provide for special measures intended to promote the trade and development of developing country contracting parties. This provision was used by developing countries to establish preferential trade arrangements even where they did not meet the 'substantially-all-trade' criteria of Article XXIV
- The 1979 'Enabling Clause' or, more formally, the decision on 'differential and more favourable treatment, non-reciprocity and fuller participation of developing countries'. This Clause was negotiated during the Tokyo Round and provided legal cover for preferential trade agreements between developing countries.

The intent and effect of Part IV and the ' Enabling Clause' were to make it easier for developing countries to establish preferential economic integration arrangements among themselves or for developed countries to extend non-reciprocal preferential access to developing countries.

The pace of the formation of economic integration schemes has not been smooth. There have been two periods of great activity. The first period in the late 1950s and early 1960s, coincided with the formation of the European Economic Community (EEC) and the independence movement in much of the Third World. The second period, the late 1980s and 1990s, coincided with the intensification of the movement in Europe towards the formation of the Single Market (European Union), the formation of the North American Free Trade Area (NAFTA), and the demise of the COMECON bloc. Each period had important differences with significance for the schemes among developing countries.

The major characteristics of the integration movement in the first period were:

- The extent to which the schemes were centred in, and modelled, on Europe
- The development of integration in the old, politically independent countries of South and Central America and the newly independent countries of Africa and the Caribbean as an economic counterpart to political independence
- The opposition of the United States, the global hegemonic power, to regional economic integration and its preference for multilateralism
- Most of the first generation integration schemes in the developing world ran into difficulties as a result of the economic crises of the 1970s and early 1980s.

The second surge of economic integration has been characterised by:

- The radically changed position of the United States and its interest in promoting and participating in regional economic integration schemes
- The rapid rate of formation of regional economic integration schemes and their overlapping membership; almost every WTO member is now a member of at least one CU or Free Trade agreement
- The number of reciprocal schemes being formed by Europe, including those developing countries in Eastern Europe, the Mediterranean, and North Africa
- The growth of mega economic integration schemes. These include Europe, now expanding to incorporate Eastern Europe, the negotiations for a Western Hemisphere Scheme (to incorporate North, Central and South America and the Caribbean), and an Asia/Pacific Scheme (to incorporate East Asia, the Pacific and North America). It is highly probable that with the demise of apartheid in Africa and the resolution of political conflicts, the Organisation of African Unity will shift focus to continental economic integration in an effort to incorporate the increasing number of overlapping regional schemes emerging on the continent
- The increasing number of economic integration schemes involving developed and developing countries
- The greater and more explicit commitment in economic integration schemes to be consistent with the WTO and to use WTO commitments as the floor from which to build.

Globalisation and Regional Integration Particularly among Developing Countries

There are some critical features of the globalisation process and the new phase of regional integration which hold great significance for developing countries. In order to fully appreciate these we need to consider the main rationale for the creation of economic integration groupings, especially among developing countries. These include:

- The economic objective of creating a large economic space within which economic operations can be given advantages and incentives which are not extended to third country competitors
- The political objective of creating an arrangement within which participating states could develop concerted positions in negotiations with third countries or the rest of the world

- The opportunity to obtain 'uncompensated, non-reciprocal' advantages in the markets of developed countries which are not available to third countries, even other developing countries.

Globalisation has undermined the first and third objectives in a number of fundamental ways. Firstly, the Uruguay Round has required all countries, developed and developing, to reduce tariffs on imports from third countries, eliminate non-tariff measures, and a range of incentives considered discriminatory. This complemented and codified, as an international binding obligation, unilateral efforts at liberalisation which were already being forced by the multilateral financial institutions (MFIs), in particular the Bretton Woods institutions, and the major bilateral donors. Tariff reductions were much more important for developing countries than the major developed countries in the Uruguay Round since the levels were already very low for the latter group.

Second, there was a strong challenge to Part IV of the GATT and to 'special and differential treatment' for developing countries granted in accordance with the 'Enabling Clause'. Whilst the concepts survived, they have been severely challenged, and are likely to be even more vigorously opposed in the next round. A major implication is that in an era of mega economic integration schemes, developing countries – including small and vulnerable ones – will not only be forced to participate with developed countries but to extend reciprocal benefits to them. This implies that developing countries in these regional integration arrangements will be extending superior conditions to economic actors, including giant transnational corporations, in developed economies than to economic actors in other developing economies, including very small ones. This is already the case with Mexico and the small countries in Central America and the Caribbean in relation to the United States of America and Canada.

Third, with lower levels of protection, the size of the economic space needed to provide meaningful incentives will increase. This will have the effect of reinforcing the tendency towards larger groupings and increasing the pressure on existing small groupings such as CARICOM.

As was indicated earlier, there is a tendency toward the formation of larger regional and even continental integration schemes involving developed and developing countries being stimulated largely by the globalisation process. This tendency will significantly undermine the capacity of regional integration groupings to function as negotiating platforms for developing countries in international negotiations.

The tendency towards large groupings to facilitate the transnational corporations could lead to a Free Trade Area involving Europe and North America. This is not a theoretical concept. It was first mooted by Jean Chrétien, Prime Minister of Canada. The possibility has since been raised both by the United States and the European Union. The formation of such a grouping involving the two major economic areas of the North would put great strain on economic groupings in the South whose members have a preferential economic relationship with either or both of these groups.

Concluding Observation

Regional economic integration groupings will face a number of significant challenges in the future in seeking to maintain their viability in the context of the unrelenting pace of globalisation. To be sure, increased cooperation among the various integration groupings could serve to bolster their capacity to determine the terms of their engagement in an increasingly liberalised global economic system.

9

The Impact of Globalisation
on the Caribbean

JESSICA BYRON

This analysis is based primarily on the experiences of the microstates of the Caribbean, namely the smallest of the small states, those with populations of 1.5 million or less, as defined by the United Nations. Most of these states can be found within the Organisation of Eastern Caribbean States sub-regional grouping.

First, I wish to make some general comments on the phenomenon of globalisation. The definition used in this paper is taken from J.A. Scholte (1997). He emphasises the tremendous changes that have taken place in the deregulation of financial markets and the exponential growth in transborder financial transactions; the increase in transnational production of goods and services and the liberalisation of international trade; the growing number of transnational enterprises (40,000 in 1995), and the trend towards the global organisation of civil society movements, corporate entities, criminal groups and regulatory bodies; the impact of communications technology on the mobility of people, ideas and cultural goods; and finally, a rapid rise in the incidence of globalised environmental problems.

Despite disagreement over what is encompassed in the globalisation phenomenon, most people accept that there have been qualitative, permanent changes in transnational relations and in the organisation and capabilities of the state. Hilbourne Watson (1994) and Scholte (1997) both refer to a 'fundamental transformation of human geography'. Most analysts, while eschewing the notion of the obsolescence of the state, agree that the functions of the state are being radically revised.

The political dimensions of globalisation include an accelerated surge of multilateral governance and new manifestations of marginalisation and inequity in this process. There is limited participation by large numbers of developing states and civil society actors in the new institutions and rule-based systems that are emerging in the era of globalisation (Held, 1997). Both the Commonwealth Report on Small States' Vulnerability (Commonwealth Secretariat, 1997) and recent United Nations reports conclude that globalisation is one of the greatest sources of vulnerability for small developing countries. They are obliged to undertake far-reaching economic reorientation as well as political action to ensure that they are not excluded from the production and marketing of goods and services and the decision-making structures of the new economic order and global polity.

Most developing countries, despite their vulnerability to the shocks of economic liberalisation and decreasing control over domestic economic processes, have inadequate resources to devote to devising appropriate strategies for participating effectively in the new global order. They tend to be absorbed by internal social and political instability and there is the temptation to be ever more parochial in vision and approach. Thus, the flip side of globalisation for significant sections of the world's population has been national fragmentation, endemic communal conflict, and the revindication of smaller and smaller territorial or group identities by those who feel excluded from, or threatened by, the processes of globalisation. Caribbean countries have experienced some of these difficulties, as is evidenced by the cases of St Kitts and Nevis or Guyana.

There are those who argue that neither vulnerability nor globalisation itself are particularly new experiences for Caribbean countries. Indeed, the population of the region was introduced during the creation of a global capitalist economy from the 1500s onwards and Caribbean peoples have shown both resilience and resourcefulness in adapting to the vicissitudes of the global economy ever since. Likewise, Caribbean countries have wrestled with the specific vulnerabilities associated with being small island developing states since their independence some 20 to 30 years ago. Their foreign policies and diplomacy have focused on negotiating appropriate international conditions and building alliances and market relationships that would facilitate their economic survival and development. In the main, the formulae consisted of negotiating non-reciprocal preferential trade agreements in as many metropolitan markets as possible, getting access to concessionary development financing, attempting to diversify both their trade and their trading partners, and constructing regional functional co-operation.

These efforts were largely successful. For the OECS, 1980-90 constituted the first decade of their independence. In the context of the international economic environment of that time, their growth rates ranged from 4.3 per cent per annum to 6.7 per cent per annum (OECS Economic Affairs Secretariat, 1994). This growth was based first and foremost on preferential trade arrangements in agricultural commodities with the European Union and on concessionary financing. However, it should be noted that their sources of revenue also included migrant remittances, offshore financial activities, offshore educational facilities, tourism, export processing zones and, in one case (St Vincent and the Grenadines), functioning as a flag of convenience state for the registration of shipping. Already by 1990, the non-government service sector contributed an average of 44 per cent of their GDP. By 1996, this figure had risen to 50 per cent of GDP.

So, while the protective buffers of preferential trade and development aid were important in the 1980s, Caribbean microstate economies and societies were already cashing in on a number of offshore and service sector opportunities that were spin-offs from globalisation. As far as the role of the state in the management of this process was concerned, most of the OECS were engaged in implementing, in varying degrees, reductions in the size of their public sector. Government regulation as well as administrative capacity remained limited except in those areas where subregional integration could create a pool of technical expertise (V. Lewis in Dominguez, Pastor and Worrell, 1993: 108, World Bank CGCED Report No. 12758 LAC, May 1994).

In the 1990s, several elements of the equation have changed. In the international economy, processes of globalisation and liberalisation have intensified, leading to marked reductions in the levels of protection accorded to the OECS in their international and regional trade. Earnings from commodity trade and concessionary financial flows have shrunk while the economies have switched to a deepening reliance on tourism, the offshore financial sector and remittances. From 1990–96, the OECS regional growth rate averaged 2.4 per cent per annum in contrast to 5.7 per cent per annum during the 1980s. The OECS state apparatus struggles to find the administrative and technical capacity to perform the roles of the regulatory state and the competitor state dictated by global neoliberalism. At the same time, state and society come under growing social and political stress as resources become scarcer and the state can no longer provide a buffer against the shocks of adjusting to the external economy. The most serious challenges will be confronted during the next five years as preferential European markets for bananas and sugar dwindle even further. The OECS countries will also be forced into a complete and painful overhaul of their taxation systems as trade liberalisation at the global, hemispheric, and regional levels comes increasingly into effect. Currently, approximately 50 per cent of tax revenues are derived from international trade taxes.

Thus far, Caribbean microstates have managed to 'tread water' in the increasingly deep and treacherous currents of globalisation. The overall picture, however, is one of growing vulnerability to external forces over which they have no control, and to which they cannot adapt quickly enough. On the positive side, they have demonstrated a capacity to exploit, at least temporarily, some niches in globalised service markets and to generate a degree of prosperity for their small populations. However, they remain extremely vulnerable to global shifts and fluctuations in tourism and off-shore financial flows. In the case of the latter, for example, there are indications in the OECD and the European Union that regulatory measures are being formulated that may curb or completely eliminate opportunities for operating offshore financial jurisdictions (*Financial Times*, 1998; CLAA Caribbean Regional Trade Brief Electronic Bulletin on Offshore Jurisdictions, May 13, 1999). Tourism will always be heavily dependent both on domestic stability and price competitiveness, and on economic conditions in the countries of origin.

Nonetheless, there is the urgent need for the OECS to adopt measures designed to strengthen their competitiveness in these and other service sectors. Moreover, although it acts as a two-edged sword, the geographical location of small Caribbean states near to the North American metropoles is an advantage in the era of globalisation. Despite the supreme challenge of negotiating mutually acceptable political and economic relationships, with the United States in particular, proximity means that they can never be totally marginalised in the global economy. Geographical proximity has time and again afforded Caribbean households and individuals survival strategies in times of economic hardship.

On the negative side, the agricultural sectors which have guaranteed employment and social peace for many years, are now the victims of global trade liberalisation. The disruption of banana marketing arrangements with the European Union offers the dismal prospect of social and political upheaval. Another negative scenario concerns the extent to which the small states of the Caribbean, based on their location, have been made part of the operational environment of globalised criminal activity – narcotrafficking – with its tremendous potential for the corruption and destabilisation of their societies. Yet another negative factor is the growing evidence of Caribbean loss of diplomatic ground and marginalisation within the new governance structures of a globalised economy. Within the WTO, for example, these countries have been reduced to waging guerrilla war on the periphery of the consultation and decision-making processes between the major actors, the EU and the US. This comes at a time when it is clearly evident that their economies and societies still require an enabling external environment, generated by appropriate international structures and policies, in order to survive. This message therefore has to be preached exhaustively by accomplished diplomats using appropriate coalitions and alliances, in all multilateral fora as well as in bilateral relations.

Finally, many argue that the rising incidence of environmental disasters at the end of the twentieth century is a consequence of the capitalist model of economic development pursued over the last fifty years, culminating in this era of globalisation. In the 1990s, certainly, a big negative factor for the Caribbean states, large and small, has been their high exposure to environmental disasters. Hurricanes, droughts, earthquakes and volcanoes have all wreaked economic and social havoc in the Caribbean Basin. In seeking to address these challenges, Caribbean microstates would need to devise new strategies.

First it would be necessary to rethink the role of the state and reapportion administrative, technical and management responsibilities among national governments, regional agencies and other actors/interest groups in the societies. The aim should be to maximise communication and co-ordination and also to maximise utilisation of whatever limited human and financial resources the societies possess.

In addition, there is the need for more thoughtful and detailed exploration of the role of the state in the context of very small Caribbean societies. There is certainly the need for significantly higher levels of state regulation in areas like the financial sector or environmental protection. However, the state also has a major role to play in human resource development, in stimulating further infrastructural development and in cushioning adjustment effects so as to prevent societal disintegration.

Action will be necessary at the international level to complement domestic and sub-regional actions and to forge diplomatic scenarios. Many analyses of globalisation speak of the transformation of human geography and the greater complexity of socio-spatial relations. I would like to refer to a different type of transformation of geography – the radically altered diplomatic landscapes that Caribbean microstates face in the era of globalisation and the consequent need to drastically rethink their diplomatic strategies and their international relations. A few key issues in this process are signalled below.

For countries such as the OECS, there is a need to put much greater emphasis on the quality and the training of foreign affairs personnel. While they should continue to organise and deploy their resources on a regional basis, they need to recruit more people with a different mix of skills and to deploy a greater number of them in different places, for example, in the WTO, and Central and South America.

A significant dimension of globalisation is regionalisation. If the hemispheric region will ultimately evolve as the main locus of economic activity for many of these countries, more resources will have to be invested in strengthening diplomatic and commercial representational networks within this area for the long term. It does not mean that the small Caribbean States will not continue to have periodic conflicts of interest with their hemispheric neighbours in the North, the Centre and the South. However, it does mean that they will gradually develop the bases of co-operation, the means to advance beyond the conflicts when they do arise, the knowledge to better exploit whatever limited means of leverage they may possess, and to determine what are realistically the areas of common ground and common interest that can be pursued.

This is no longer an epoch purely of state-to-state diplomacy. Given the reduced capacity and resources of the state and the far wider scope of diplomatic activity, small Caribbean societies have to ensure that their business sectors participate vigorously in all business, for example, the ACP business forum and the FTAA business forum, and that information and dialogue flow freely between the state sector and business interests. Likewise, another key area for transnational relations concerns the activities of civil society. Local Non Governmental Organisations (NGOs), the state and NGOs from other developing countries as well as developed countries can often join forces on certain issues, to their mutual advantage. This has been explored with the EU NGDOs on the banana market issue, using the rallying cry of fair trade. Another issue in which such an alliance of interests was evidenced was in the scuttling of the MAI negotiations within the OECD, mainly by the actions of NGOs, in a forum in which developing-country voices were excluded. Where possible, alliances with transnational civil society must be built, going through the channels of civil society in the national and regional context.

Finally, it is increasingly evident that the present patterns of liberalisation and globalisation are running into crisis and are being called into question. Just as in the early 1970s, we are approaching another important psychological and strategic moment in North-South relations. There is growing discussion about the prevailing institutions and rules of global governance. Very constructively for Caribbean small states, some of this debate has raised issues regarding the protective mechanisms that should be introduced or reintroduced into international institutions and global policy regimes to accommodate the needs and interests of small and vulnerable societies. Caribbean microstates have a strategic imperative to orient their diplomatic and intellectual resources towards stimulating and spreading this debate as far as possible, and forging all the necessary alliances to push through the necessary reforms in multilateral institutions and in global economic policies and norms.

In conclusion, I do not believe that we can reconstruct Southern solidarity in quite the same form or with the same approaches as in the 1970s. The world is much more complex, composite and fragmented: globalisation, regionalism, small states, big emerging markets, LLDCs, collapsing states, the unknown elements and actors of East and Central Europe and of Central Asia, the voluminous technical rules of the WTO or the Kyoto Protocol – all of these new landscapes and scenarios are powerful reasons to go back to the diplomatic drawing board and do our homework, prepare ourselves as never before, as we never had to in the 1970s. We can only begin to identify pragmatically the very limited areas of common interest where there is real scope for South-South solidarity when we have thoroughly analysed and understood our own interests and the interests of the actors in the hemispheric context in which we are located.

References

Caribbean Latin American Action, Caribbean Regional Trade Brief – Offshore Jurisdictions, May 13, 1999.

Commonwealth Advisory Group, *A Future for Small States: Overcoming Vulnerability* (Commonwealth Secretariat, London, 1997).

'The EURO', *The Financial Times, (London: Financial Times, 1998).*

D. Held, 'Globalisation and Democracy', *Global Governance*, Vol. 3, No. 3, 1997.

Klak, T., ed., *Globalisation and Neoliberalism: the Caribbean Context* (London: Rowman and Littlefield, 1998).

V. Lewis, 'The Eastern Caribbean States: Fledgling Sovereignties in the Global Environment', in Dominguez, J., R. Pastor, R.D. Worrell, eds., *Democracy in the Caribbean* (Baltimore: Johns Hopkins University Press, 1993, pp. 99–121).

OECS Trade Statistics Digest, Vol. 3, 1994.

J.A. Scholte, 'Global Capitalism and the State', *International Affairs*, Vol. 73, No. 3, 1997.

Watson, H., *The Caribbean in the Global Political Economy* (Kingston, Jamaica: Ian Randle, 1994).

The World Bank CGCED, Report No. 12758 LAC, 'Economic Policies for Transition in the Organisation of Eastern Caribbean States', May 1994.

10

Globalisation and the Private Sector

CHARLES ROSS

Introduction

Globalisation is now blamed for many ills and is viewed by some as the new threat to the prosperity and growth of developing countries. I would like to propose that for a moment we focus instead on the opportunities that may come with globalisation and explore ways of exploiting those opportunities for the benefit of our countries and the people who inhabit them.

The Opportunities of Globalisation

One of the more controversial features of globalisation has been the tremendous increase in the volume and speed of the flows of private capital between countries. There has been much criticism of this feature of international capital markets since the withdrawal of funds from emerging markets in South-East Asia set off the crisis in those economies. However, there were no complaints when the original inflows of those funds were fuelling the high rates of growth that occurred in those countries prior to their current difficulties. The fact that some developing countries have benefited in the past from the capital inflows brought about by globalisation, means that those countries and others can benefit again in the future, if the lessons of the recent past are learnt and learnt well.

The bottom line is that there are capital surpluses in the industrialised countries of the North, which are seeking returns that are higher than those which can be obtained in their home markets. There is a shortage of capital in the developing countries of the South, which also have large resources of relatively cheap labour available for employment. Globalisation therefore offers tremendous opportunities for the coming together of the capital and technology of the North and the labour and natural resources of the South, to increase employment, output, and living standards in the developing countries.

The increased openness of markets in the industrialised countries – another feature of globalisation – will provide the market access for the goods which are produced from this investment in the developing countries. The challenge for developing countries is to so organise their domestic economies that they are, or become, attractive locations for investment in the production of internationally competitive goods and services.

The Imperatives for Developing Economies

The creation of a local environment that will encourage investment in productive and export-oriented enterprises will require responsible and consistent macro-economic policies which do not distort prices and re-source allocation in the domestic economy. These policies must not be biased in favour of consumption, but must encourage domestic saving and investment. Policies that favour consumption may end by attracting inflows of the so-called hot money - short-term inflows which are in search of high interest earnings, rather than investment in longer-term productive activity. The sudden withdrawal of such funds (together with the interest earned) has precipitated large currency movements in a number of emerging markets in recent years. The greatest danger for developing countries at present, is that they allow themselves to be convinced by the multilateral lending agencies to incur huge hard currency loans to prop up their currencies, in effect bailing out the international investors who gambled on the high domestic interest rates with their 'hot money'.

This huge debt burden will then act as a brake on the country's prospects for economic growth for many years to come and will create a moral hazard problem for the international portfolio investors who then expect to get the benefits of high interest rates in emerging economies without any of the attendant risks. Having been spared their losses in one market, they are then free to seek out similar opportunities elsewhere, with all the attendant problems for the countries concerned. Investors must take their losses or be bailed out by the countries from which their investments originate.

Globalisation is a natural outgrowth of capitalist economic systems (Marx's cycle of capital hinted at it decades ago) and attempting to resist it or turn it back may be like the Luddites attempting to halt the industrial revolution. There are definite potential advantages for developing countries, and we may be well advised to see how we can take the best advantage of it rather than trying to halt it in its tracks. Capital controls on outflows are certainly not the way to go, since investors are unlikely to bring their money into a country in the first place, if they are unable to take it out when they wish to do so. We must also bear in mind the fact that developing countries are in need of capital to develop their productive and social infrastructure and that foreign direct investment is perhaps the most constructive avenue through which we can attract such capital.

The Real Threats of Globalisation

Globalisation does, however, change the international playing field, and in that respect it could be considered to carry some threats for developing countries, at least in so far as it changes their traditional relationships with the industrialised countries of the North. In the first instance, we must accept that we cannot base our development on the preferential access of traditional commodities to their accustomed markets in Western Europe and North America. Commodity production will continue to falter as a development option. The terms of trade will continue to deteriorate with respect to commodities. Mendicancy is no longer an option. Reciprocal trade is the way of the future. We must get into the production of tradable goods and services on an internationally competitive basis.

We must accept that growth and development will have to come at least initially from a rational and efficient allocation of domestic resources and that this will only take place in a context of rational macro-economic policies. These policies must allocate resources to the areas of the economy which will earn the highest returns, and in small open economies these areas should be those parts of the economy that are producing goods and services for sale to international markets. In poor countries where capital is scarce, it is all the more important that resources are allocated rationally and to areas of economic activity that will lead to sustainable development and which will not create a dependency on international charity for the maintenance of external and internal stability.

In short, policies must be geared towards encouraging savings and investment rather than consumption. An integral part of such an environment will include a small and efficient government which maintains balance in its operations so that it does not crowd out the private sector and allow that sector access to sufficient resources to finance high rates of investment and economic growth. We also need to accept that high rates of economic growth are the only sustainable route to poverty reduction in our countries, and this will only be achieved if the appropriate macroeconomic policies are put in place and kept in place over a long period of time.

Finally, we must be prepared to examine the issues carefully and determine what is in our interest as a country, and not allow ourselves to be manipulated by international interests that are quite capable of looking after themselves. We must realise that as poor, capital-deficient countries, it cannot be in our interest to restrict the inflow of capital into our economies. We must also accept that it is our responsibility to so order our domestic policies that the capital that enters our countries does so to take advantage of investment opportunities in the productive sector, and that as little as possible enters as speculative short-term capital. Where such capital does enter our market, we must be prepared to allow the investors to reap the benefit of their investments when they are profitable and also to bear the cost of their losses when they are not. At the end of the day, we must not fear the market as an allocator of resources – it may not be perfect but, in my humble opinion, a better one is yet to be found.

Conclusion

The analyses contained in the various articles included in this volume have succeeded in shedding light on a number of aspects of globalisation. It would be useful, by way of conclusion therefore, to highlight some of the central elements that might form the basis of a strategy to be pursued by the developing countries in response to the challenges presented by globalisation.

At the philosophical level, the developing countries need to counter the intellectual hegemony of the North, based on neo-classical economic orthodoxy, by articulating an alternative vision of development that will lead to a more democratic global economic order. Such an initiative on the part of the developing countries is urgently necessary in order to move beyond the 'Washington Consensus' which has clearly not served the interests of the developing countries.

In this context, the developing countries need to maintain their solidarity in the negotiations on international economic issues in the various multilateral forums in which such negotiations take place. However, given the increased heterogeneity of the Group of 77 based on differences in ideological perspectives and also levels of development, some commentators have questioned the viability of the group as a mechanism for promoting co-operation among the developing countries. Although it is true that differences do exist within the Group, for example, in terms of the attitude of individual countries to liberalisation, the developing countries are nevertheless linked together by the fact that, by and large, the functioning of the international economic system places them at a distinct disadvantage *vis-à-vis* the developed countries. In any event, these countries will be placed at an even greater disadvantage if they opt to 'go it alone'.

Moreover, given the increased importance of the multilateral trade negotiations taking place within the WTO in shaping the structure of international economic relations, the developing countries need to ensure increased co-ordination of their positions on the various issues under negotiation. Although in keeping with the convention within the GATT – which was the predecessor organisation of the WTO – the developing countries have not traditionally operated as the Group of 77, the overriding importance of the issues suggest that the Group should play a more active role in formulating broad principles designed to shape the substantive content of the negotiations. This does not necessarily mean locking all countries into specific and detailed positions acceptable to the Group of 77, since it may be necessary to provide a degree of flexibility for individual countries, given the binding nature of the commitments of the WTO. However, there is an obvious need for agreement among the developing countries on broad strategic objectives in order to ensure that they do not operate at cross purposes by pursuing contradictory initiatives.

More particularly, the developing countries should continue to oppose negotiations within the WTO on new issues such as competition policy, environment and labour standards and procurement, on the terms proposed by the developed countries, until a review of the implications of the existing agreements is carried out and a commitment made, on this basis, to modify as appropriate, provisions contained in such agreements that are clearly detrimental to the economic interests of the developing countries.

In a similar vein, efforts should continue to be made to oppose the proposed Multilateral Agreement on Investment (MAI), originally promoted by the developed countries and currently held in abeyance, but which could surface again in the future. In fact, the attempt to use the MAI as an instrument to confer national treatment on foreign investors represents a clear attempt to subordinate the national development objectives of the developing countries to the needs of such investors.

In general, in approaching the negotiations on international trade issues, it is important for the developing countries to defend the principle of special and differential treatment, in view of the fact that, given the comparatively low level of development of the majority of the developing countries and the undifferentiated nature of the structure of their economies which tends to be biased towards primary commodity production, these countries will be unable to compete effectively in a fully liberalised trading regime. The developing countries must nevertheless seek to improve their efficiency and competitiveness through the introduction of new and innovative methods of production designed to promote productivity growth.

At the same time, the developing countries should continue to oppose the current undemocratic procedures which govern the negotiations within the WTO and insist on more open participation for all member states of the organisation. More specifically, the so called 'green room' process, which is based on the arbitrary selection of member states to participate in the negotiations on specific issues to the exclusion of the wider membership of the organisation, should be discontinued and replaced by a more open-ended system of negotiations in which all countries would be free to participate in keeping with their particular interest in the issues under negotiation. This should not exclude the possibility of identifying spokes-persons for the developing countries as a whole or even for the various geographical regions, selected by the countries themselves on the under-standing nevertheless that all number states would be free to be present at the negotiations.

In terms of the functioning of the Group of 77 itself, there has been a tendency in recent years for some member countries with a more conser-vative bent to oppose the adoption of a common Group of 77 position on certain issues under negotiation with the developed countries. This often leads to a stalemate on such issues or the adoption of an approach that is almost neutral on particular issues. The working procedure of the Group therefore needs to be modified in order to ensure its more efficient opera-tion. To this end, the principle of consensus, which implies an interpretation by the Chairperson of the Group of the overwhelming sentiment of the Group, should be asserted instead of the principle of unanimity. The latter would in effect confer a veto power on a small number of countries, which could clearly operate to the detriment of the overwhelming majority of developing countries. In this scenario, individual countries which wish to dissent from the consensus should be allowed to express their reservations on the issue.

More generally, given the experience of the East Asian crisis which, it is conceded, was caused mainly by the rapid inflow and outflow of speculative capital which sent shock waves throughout the international financial system, the developing countries should introduce appropriate prudential regulations to manage such flows. They would also need to continue to press for a restructuring of existing arrangements centred on the IMF and for the creation of new international financial architecture capable of providing financial support to the developing countries in need of such assistance on an urgent basis. This should be implemented with less insistence on policy conditionalities based on an adherence to restrictive policy prescriptions inspired by neo-liberal economic principles, as opposed to a more expansionary and structurally oriented macroeconomic policy framework. The new system should also incorporate an early warning system that could alert countries to possible dangers likely to arise either from particular domestic economic policies or from speculative attacks on their economies from external sources.

Moreover, the new international financial architecture should be based on a democratic decision-making process in which the developing countries could participate on a more equitable basis *vis-à-vis* the developed countries, bearing in mind that the international financial system impacts on all countries, whereas, at present, the developing countries are largely excluded from the decision-making process on the major global economic issues. In other words, under the existing system, the economic fortunes of the developing countries are significantly influenced by the decisions taken by the developed countries which adopt policies within the restricted framework of the Group of 7, which in turn influence the policy orientation of the international financial institutions.

As stated earlier, the process of globalisation has been accompanied by a conscious effort to marginalise the organisations of the UN system in order to prevent them from standing in the way of this process. This has been particularly true in the case of UNCTAD which, in the past, had played a leading role in providing analyses, formulating policy positions and, generally, supporting the efforts of the developing countries in their quest for development. Indeed, in recent years, a concerted effort has been made by the developed countries in the context of globalisation to confine decision-making on important international economic issues to the IMF, the World Bank and, since 1995, the WTO, which now act as a triad of forces shaping global economic relations.

The growing marginalisation of the role of the UN has been accomplished in part by withholding resources in order to force reforms designed essentially to reorient the agenda of the organisation away from the major economic issues, thus rendering it increasingly incapable of dealing with the central issues of development. In keeping with this policy, there is increasing opposition on the part of the developed countries to the pursuit by the various organisations of independent analysis of issues, as opposed to those on which both developed and developing countries agree. This has resulted in a significant weakening of the role and influence of the Organisation in the economic sphere, and the traditional emphasis on development which has been the hallmark of the work of the Organisation over the years and which is, in fact, a principle firmly enshrined in the UN Charter. Instead, development has been subordinated to the imperatives of the market, which are premised almost exclusively on the narrow concept of allocative efficiency, which has tended to exclude the important principles of justice and equity.

Not surprisingly, despite the much-vaunted claims about the benefits of market-driven globalisation, the statistics suggest that vast segments of humanity continue to live in abject poverty and are forced to fend for survival on a daily basis in a world which has the capacity to eradicate poverty and social deprivation, if only its resources were distributed more equitably.

The assertion of a counter philosophy to current approaches to globalisation would therefore need to be premised on the restoration of the central role of the UN in respect of international economic issues, a recommitment of the international community to development, and an enlightened pattern of international development co-operation which recognises development as the primary objective of such co-operation. This would also require a renewed commitment on the part of the developed countries to provide an adequate level of ODA which has witnessed a significant decline in recent years, instead of reliance on FDI - the bulk of which has been directed to less than a dozen developing countries in East Asia and parts of Latin America and therefore has not benefited the majority of the developing countries. The achievement of these objectives will depend on the promotion of a more intensive pattern of co-operation among the developing countries in support of a strengthened negotiating capacity based on the adoption of a strategic programme of action shaped by a clearly articulated vision of development and international development co-operation.

However, since the ability to effect change in the global economic system is essentially linked to the exercise of power, the efforts of the developing countries to counter the current approach to globalisation would need to be bolstered by a conscious policy to build a countervailing economic power. Consequently, a concerted effort should be made by the developing countries to promote industrial complementarity based on the establishment of joint production enterprises, geared to the exploitation of their natural resources and other endowments, in an effort to localise value-added by facilitating the exploitation of such resources. Such arrangements have the potential not only to fundamentally alter the pattern of resource use in the international system, but also to reorient the structure of their economies away from the traditional dependence on primary commodity production towards new forms of manufacturing and also towards services which have assumed increasing importance in light of the increased 'tertierisation' of the global economy and the emergence of services as the fastest-growing sector of that economy. The successful pursuit of such a strategy will also need to pay special attention to the application of new and innovative technologies in the development process, and also the development of an adequate level of human resources, since both economic theory and the evidence of recent economic history have convincingly demonstrated that the application of technology and higher levels of skill formation in the economy have been the key to economic progress.

In order to complete the framework for a strategic response to globalisation, the developing countries need to strengthen the institutional mechanism necessary to follow up and implement the various decisions of the Group. While the establishment of a full-blown secretariat may not be immediately feasible, concerted efforts will need to be made to improve the institutional capability of the Group on a phased basis.

These considerations notwithstanding, it is clear that globalisation will continue its inexorable march in the years ahead. However, its content and orientation are likely to undergo significant modification as a result of the dual impact of the theoretical challenge mounted by the developing countries, and also the objective economic forces which are likely to influence the evolution of the global economy. Hopefully this volume will contribute not only to the theoretical exposition of the phenomenon, but also to the identification of a number of practical proposals that will help to shape a practical action oriented agenda to be pursued by the developing countries. Such an agenda is central to the effort to create an international economic system that is more humanistic in content, infused with the principles of equity and justice, and which will – hopefully – put an end to the unconscionable calculus of inequality implicit in the current Social Darwinist approach to globalisation that has kept vast segments of humanity in a state of abject poverty in the midst of a world of plenty.

Annex I

Statement at the Opening Session of Symposium

REX NETTLEFORD
Vice Chancellor of the University of the West Indies

Whether we wish it or not, the University of the West Indies has no choice but to commit itself to what is clearly a central challenge both to itself and the region it was set up to serve, for the entire region belongs to the beleagured, penurious South (Barbados notwithstanding), namely, the quest for strategic responses to the challenge of globalisation.

Judging from the list of participants, there is clearly no shortage of minds in determining such strategies. But how can we find the tactics that will close the cycle of power needed to confront the sort of forces that if allowed to reign, can leave us forever on the margin of human-scale development, prosperity, peace, and relative stability? This has been our problem for the past half-millennium, and any approach without a sense of the provenance and nature of the societies we tenant, or of the modes of relating between such societies, on the one hand, and the traditionally better off (materially speaking) countries concentrated in the North Atlantic, on the other, is not likely to take us very far.

Happily, nothing has quite stood still, though many things have apparently remained tenaciously the same. We now have the capacity and capability to meet and think and discuss, with clear plans for continuing participation in similar exercises, starting with the G-15 meetings just around the corner, the South Summit planned for Havana during the early months of the new millennium and our own projected effort on the Mona

Globalisation: A Calculus of Inequality

Campus, at the beginning of Semester 1 of the 1999-2000 academic year. There can be hope in and beyond the would-be despair. I see these international initiatives as part of the strategy of inclusion of the stake-holding South in global discussions designed to find ways to preserve the stability and equity of the international and financial system. Without such stability and equity, the disadvantaged South will never be able to re-position itself in the new order, let alone hold a position advantageous to itself.

Our future has to be seriously understood, not only in terms of contemporary realities, but also in terms of the nature of things as they have been for more than a lifetime of human endeavour in this business of trading, manipulating money transactions, and concocting deals across geographical boundaries. One thing is certain in all of this: it is people who are doing these things, not systems and procedures which, after all, are themselves the brainchild of people.

On the lips of everyone today is this phenomenon called 'globalisation' which, to many, describes the end-of-century feature of a world order marked by rapid growth in world trade, direct foreign investment, and cross-border financial flows, determining the developing countries' continuing disadvantaged location in that world order. Some feel that it replaces the old tyrannies of slavery, imperialism, colonialism, and communism. I certainly regard it as a twenty-first century version of the old global vision of Planet Earth as a cake to be sliced and shared among clever bidders, a vision which guided the exploitation beginning 500 years ago, of new lands and slave labour, which established empires and prepared the world for division into rich (who now act in concert) and poor, between developed and developing, between the technologically advanced and the rest – a condition which globalisation, as we now know it, serves to reinforce and sustain. Without an understanding of this context, we are not likely to be able to answer the question of urgency embedded in the theme of this symposium.

Even the rich are having second thoughts about the virtues of liberalisation as it has manifested itself. And we in the University of the West Indies need to take heed and be careful that we do not get trapped yet again in a hand-me-down discourse which is being discarded by the very people who first wore the clothing elsewhere. We here at UWI must avoid what could be mistaken as intellectual minstrelsy in terms of market-driven neo-liberalist advocates battling with closet socialists or doctrinaire statists. These polarities have less to do with us than we think.

One would have thought that the problems of South East Asia, which now impact on the world's economy, would teach us some lessons. I hope this symposium will reflect on the loss of teeth by these Asian tigers which wise men for two decades have been telling us should be the models for all the South in pursuit of growth and development. The IMF, that awesome International Ministry of Finance, as Julius Nyerere once dubbed it, is now broke.

Like a hurricane, the IMF and all other Bretton Woods agents of fury have had us bobbing and weaving in the whirlwind. What is necessary is that we must stand firm (no partisan political pun intended) so that after the breeze blows, the plant can take spring again because the roots are deep-delved. This is not metaphor; it is the kind of hard-nosed reality we must expect from the responses by the private sector, the government, the educational system, and the people at large – all in alliance.

A close study of all those societies once considered prosperous, and which we admired, will show that all those stakeholders I have just mentioned approached their problems in those countries on the basis of periods of conscious collaboration rooted in mutual trust. I recommend it for our serious consideration as tactics and strategy.

Admittedly, there is evidence of the continuing success of free capital flows in a place like Hong Kong (though even that marvel of a joint has not been without its problems); but we must also admit the spectacular nature of the crashes that have followed the liberalised trail. Brazil is teetering at the moment, we hear.

I say all this to bring us back around to the responsibilities we have to and for ourselves in this game. Understanding the nature of the business is paramount. But so is the will to use that understanding in designing a strategy of teamwork first within nations and secondly between nations in the South and with other stakeholders in the business.

A few years ago, I advised with a dinosaur's savvy that our aim should be the unleashing of entrepreneurial energy for the development of the productive forces, with greater emphasis on facilitating private capital accumulation as a major instrument of economic production, instead of having the State as such a prime player. The proven inadequacy of the State's ability to deliver justifies the State's withdrawal from this sphere of economic development. But the 'no less proven' tendency of a concentration of oligarchic economic power when capital accumulation and production are left unregulated in the hands of private monopolies, advises caution and dictates the forging of appropriate, innovative, flexible, and responsive mechanisms to mitigate the excesses of greed and cynicism and to temper unbridled enthusiasm for rapid bottom-line success at any cost. That was what I said in 1992.

Greed, cynicism and unbridled enthusiasm for bottom-line success at any cost have certainly caught up with us in the South. That so many of us have let down the side in Jamaica, and no doubt elsewhere, is impatient of debate. Few of us can with any conscience throw stones at the fellows in Jamaica House, since our House is also made of glass. But this is not the time for charges and counter-charges.

We are all we have; we must get on with the job, working together. The culture of partnership is a possible modality for action and the University of the West Indies together with like institutions throughout the 'Two-Thirds World' must commit itself to membership in this partnership between Government, private sector, and the community which we all serve, and all in partnership with regional compatriots in the South. The knowledge economy which is upon us demands no less.

Moreover,

> . . . such tri-partite, co-ordinated approach to governance [public or private governance] deserves serious application [and consideration] consonant with the aspirations of participatory democracy and the optimisation of productivity for a well educated, highly skilled, and culturally confident human resource base.

That is what a Government Committee of Advisors on Government Structure advised the Government of Jamaica in 1992. A parallel recommendation for countries in the region (and by implication for countries in the South) is to be found in *Time For Action*, the West Indian Commission Report which I hope Sir Alister McIntyre will revisit later in this seminar.

Such are the attributes which serve as magnet for the serious investment after which we hanker, even when the investment that parades itself is the proverbial 'hot money'. Behind this must be the creativity, innovative spirit, negotiating prowess, hard work, and imagination.

How else can we meet the crises to establish safety net programmes to protect the most vulnerable segments of populations in the South? Does this make any sense to us who are now in feverish quest for economic growth and sustainable development? The answer remains in our hands and no one else's. For creatively claiming that sense of ownership for both our problems and the solutions, is no less a strategic response to globalisation.

Annex II

Statement at the Opening Session of Symposium

RUDY INSANALLY
Ambassador, Chairman Group of 77 (1999)

I was truly delighted by the invitation to participate in this International Symposium on 'Globalisation – A Strategic Response from the South'. It offered an opportunity not only to escape from the cold of New York for some Caribbean sunshine, but also to renew ties with my alma mater, the sponsor of the Symposium. I did not hesitate for a moment to accept.

However, as a layman among specialists, I cannot pretend to offer any special wisdom on the issue at hand. The most I can hope to do is to make some general observations from a United Nations perspective. As the Chairman of the Group of 77 and China, I would like to think that the views which I express today are shared to some degree by the membership. I should like, however, to issue the caveat that I speak for myself and not on their behalf.

A preliminary remark could be that globalisation is now, for better or worse, a reality of our times. The term has entered the economic lexicon and, indeed, has become part of our daily jargon. However, though freely bandied about by just about everyone, its meaning is often very elusive, changing constantly depending on the context in which it is used. Not unlike its climatic companion, El Niño, globalisation is not fully understood, and yet is readily invoked to explain almost every development in the world economy. However, whatever may be our individual views on the subject, we can all agree on one thing: that the development prospects of the countries of the South have become increasingly intertwined with this phenomenon, and will continue to be determined by its influence. For this reason, we would do well to study closely its nature and impact in order to determine how best it may be harnessed for our good.

All the evidence available to us thus far demonstrates that, fuelled by the technology revolution and the increasing liberalisation of trade and finance, the process of globalisation is rapidly transforming the world into a global marketplace. As its effects continue to impinge on the daily lives of people everywhere, the process itself has engendered a sense of helplessness and a loss of control. Sovereignty is being redefined as national governments are marginalised and supranational forces become ascendant.

This latter development is perhaps the most disconcerting aspect of the process. For while the implications of decision-making transcend national borders, becoming increasingly global, the key decision-makers are, for the most part, concentrated in a few major industrialised countries. Yet, the effects of their decisions are felt from one end of the globe to the other, touching the lives of millions of people. These are the poor and weak who are on the margins of these developments, and whose fate is now subject to manipulation through the marvels of modern technology, as financial flows are moved in and out of economies, literally at the push of a button.

The East Asian crisis has graphically illustrated the perils of the current environment. Many countries are now likely to recede further into the backwaters of poverty as the gains resulting from the past decades of economic growth are dramatically eroded. As their number increases, so does the risk of a worldwide recession. Increasingly, there is a clamour for some order in the workings of the global economy. The existing international institutions are deemed to have failed in dealing with the underlying systemic deficiencies leading to the demands on all sides for the reform or redesign of the international financial architecture.

This exercise, to be credible, has to be an inclusive one that takes into account the concerns and needs of all states, in particular the poor and most vulnerable. These bear a disproportionate weight of adverse changes in the global economy, but yet their voices are rarely heard or acknowledged. In their Declaration of Caracas in January 1998, G-24 ministers made a number of important recommendations on this issue. These need to be systematically followed up and implemented, so that developing countries may acquire a greater role in global decision-making.

In December 1998, in responding to the growing challenge of globalisation, the United Nations General Assembly decided to place the question on the Organisation's agenda. This decision, embodied in General Assembly resolution 53/ 169: of December 15, 1998 entitled 'The Role of the United Nations in promoting development in the context of globalisation and interdependence' was premised, among other things, on the recognition that the UN as a universal forum, was in a unique position to promote international co-operation on these matters. It is for the United Nations, for the international community as a whole, and for the developing world especially, to address this central challenge of our times.

These realities demand creative thinking and urgent action. To move forward, the developing world needs to undertake an in-depth appraisal of both the opportunities and risk associated with globalisation. We already know that the experience of globalisation within the South has been mixed. Some countries have been more successful than others in integrating with the global economy. For far too many, however, the experience – at least in the short term – has been negative and has led to their marginalisation or total exclusion from the benefits of the global economy. Traditional international co-operation is in sharp decline while no new mechanisms have evolved to compensate for the resulting shortfall in development resources. In these circumstances, an earnest effort has to be made to place development financing on a sound and stable footing.

Developing countries must ensure that this issue is given priority attention at the Conference on financing for development scheduled to be held no later than 2000. Not only must we seek to return the currently low levels of ODA towards previously agreed targets, but we must also negotiate for improved and increased investment flows as well as new and additional sources to provide the volume of financing required. It is not too early to begin the formulation of a strategy to arrest the slowdown of the world economy and to reposition our countries on the growth curve.

Globalisation clearly points to the need for new forms of partnership to deal with the vast array of problems that have arisen. Alone, governments find themselves unable to cope with the situation. The private sector and civil society as a whole will have to assist in keeping globalisation on an even keel. As important actors on the world scene, non-governmental organisations will have to be taken into account as we strive to lay the foundation for sustained economic growth and sustainable development in the future. Accordingly, they must be brought into the dialogue to form a strategic alliance to preserve the common good.

The growing interdependence among developing countries must now be fully harnessed to provide a new dynamic for South-South co-operation, long recognised as indispensable to the progress of the Third World. An important feature of our times, which has paralleled the process of globalisation, has been the broadening and deepening of integration processes both at the regional and sub-regional levels, including those among the countries of the South. These arrangements can offer, I believe, a useful buffer against the onslaught of unbridled global market forces, and allow countries some breathing space to pool their resources and jointly develop their productive capacities.

The G77 High-level Conference on Regional and Sub-regional Economic Co-operation held in December 1998 in Bali, Indonesia has provided a platform, through the Bali Declaration and Plan of Action, for further exploration of the potential for co-operation between regional and sub-regional economic groupings and communities of the South as well as with the private sector. The year 2000 will witness the holding of the first ever South Summit in Havana, Cuba. It will be a historic opportunity for developing countries to chart a safe course in this rapidly globalising world. We should not fail to take advantage of the Summit to concert our policies and maximise our co-operation for development.

At the same time, globalisation makes necessary and urgent a new dialogue between the developed and developing countries in search of a consensus on effective development policy. The broad divergence of policies and strategies which now prevail must be narrowed if globalisation is to be mutually advantageous. For the greater part, the developed countries appear to feel that aid to the developing world is wasteful and that only free markets, where competition thrives, can create economic and social progress. On the other hand, most developing countries see globalisation to be largely of unilateral benefit to the industrialised world and its multinational corporations. Thus, until and unless there is a meeting of the minds on a new development strategy, globalisation is likely to remain an engine with few carriages.

Our ultimate aim should be the creation of a 'new global economic order' that is just and equitable. Admittedly, some people in the developed world appear to be allergic to the mere mention of the word 'order' (witness the fate of the 'New International Economic Order' and the 'New Information Order'). Nevertheless, there does now appear to be a glimmer of political willingness to accept some form of international partnership for development. Certainly, recent statements emanating from the G-7 and the OECD/DAC would lead one to believe that this concept is being gradually accepted. If this is so, then it should be possible to begin to define, as with other partnerships, the rights and obligations of the parties. Such terms of engagement would not only provide greater predictability in international economic relations but also serve to mitigate the worst effects of globalisation.

The Caribbean is particularly well-placed during 1999 to provide leadership in the building of such a partnership. Not only does Guyana have the Chairmanship of the Group of 77 and China, but Jamaica has also spearheaded the G-15. This remarkable coincidence should inspire us as a region to create a new vision for the developing world. Regrettably, small states and their governments – like those in the Caribbean – may not have the luxury of time to be able to elaborate such ideas. There is therefore, to my mind, a useful role to be played by our institutions of higher learning in helping to develop new strategies to deal with current development needs. As we have been reminded by a prophet of old, 'Without a vision, our people will certainly perish'.

Out of this meeting should therefore come a broad definition of the region's future needs as well as a strategy by which they may be satisfied. Nothing less can be expected from this assembly of some of the best and brightest minds in the South. As its motto, *Oriens ex occidente lux*, suggests, the University can indeed provide a beacon for countries of the South as they seek safe passage through the uncharted sea of globalisation.

List of Contributors

Denis Benn is Michael Manley Professor of Public Affairs/Public Policy, University of the West Indies, Mona, Jamaica. He has had a distinguished career in the United Nations in which he has held a number of senior positions. Professor Benn has also participated in several international conferences. He has written a number of books and articles on the Caribbean and on international development issues. He is a member of the Board of Governors of the South Centre.

Richard Bernal is Jamaica's Ambassador to the United States and Permanent Representative to the Organisation of American States (OAS), based in Washington, DC. Ambassador Bernal has served the government of Jamaica in various capacities in the Central Bank and the Planning Institute of Jamaica. He was Chairman of the OAS Working Group on the Enterprise for the Americas Initiative and represented Jamaica at several international conferences. Ambassador Bernal is the author of a number of studies on economic and financial issues.

Byron Blake is Assistant Secretary General in the Caricom Secretariat located in Georgetown, Guyana in which he has had a long and distinguished career. An economist by training, Mr Blake is a well known expert on Caribbean affairs, most notably on regional economic integration.

Jessica Byron is a Lecturer in the Department of Government, University of the West Indies. Her interests are international relations theory and feminism. Dr Byron has written extensively on various aspects of international relations, with special reference to the Caribbean.

Norman Girvan is the Secretary General of the ACS located in Port-of-Spain, Trinidad and Tobago. Prior to taking up this appointment, Dr Girvan served as Professor of Development Studies and Director of the Sir Arthur Lewis Institute of Social and Economic Studies, University of the West Indies. He is a highly respected economist and author of a number of books and articles on various aspects of the Caribbean economy.

Branislav Gosovic is the Officer-in-Charge of the South Centre in Geneva. He previously served in UNCTAD, UNEP, ECLAC and in the secretariats of the Brundtland Commission and the South Commission. Dr Gosovic has written a number of books and articles on various aspects of international economic co-operation.

Rudy Insanally is Guyana's Permanent Representative to the United Nations in New York. He is also Chancellor of the University of Guyana. Ambassador Insanally is a former President of the United Nations General Assembly and served as Chairman of the Group of 77 during 1999. Ambassador Insanally has had a distinguished diplomatic career and also served as Ambassador to Venezuela, the Caribbean, and as Guyana's Permanent Representative to the European Union in Brussels.

Rex Nettleford is Vice-Chancellor of the University of the West Indies. Professor Nettleford is a prolific writer and author of a number of books, including *Rastafarianism in Jamaica* (with F.R. Augier and M.G. Smith); *Manley and the New Jamaica*; *Dance Jamaica*; *Self Definition and Artistic Discovery*; and *The University of the West Indies: A Caribbean Response to the Challenge of Change*. He is also the founder, artistic director, and principal choreographer of Jamaica's National Dance Theatre Company.

John Ohiorhenuan is the Director of the Special Unit for Technical Co-operation Among Developing Countries (TCDC), UNDP, New York. Prior to joining the UNDP, he was a Professor of Economics at the University of Ibadan in Nigeria. He also served, on secondment from UNDP, with the Global Environment Faculty (GEF) in the World Bank. Dr Ohiorhenuan has written extensively on globalisation and economic management issues with special reference to Africa.

Charles Ross is the Executive Director of the Private Sector Organisation of Jamaica (PSOJ). As Executive Director of the PSOJ, he plays a leading role in articulating ideas relevant to the concerns of the private sector. He is also the host of a radio programme which discusses issues of popular concern.

Clive Thomas is Professor of Economics and Director of the Institute of Development Studies at the University of Guyana. He recently served as the George Beckford Professor of Caribbean Economy at the University of the West Indies. Professor Thomas is a well-known Caribbean economist and has written several books and articles on economic theory and development. He has served as a consultant to a number of international organisations, including the United Nations.

Manuela Tortora is currently attached to the UNCTAD Secretariat in Geneva. Prior to taking up this appointment, Dr Tortora served with the Latin American Economic System (SELA) based in Caracas. She is an authority on international financial issues and has written extensively on the subject.

Index